TASSO
CLAVIGO

Georg Heuser
In Dankbarkeit

Johann Wolfgang von Goethe

TASSO
CLAVIGO

translated by Robert David MacDonald

OBERON BOOKS
LONDON

First published in this collection in 2003 by Oberon Books Ltd.
(incorporating Absolute Classics)
521 Caledonian Road, London N7 9RH
Tel: 020 7607 3637 / Fax: 020 7607 3629
e-mail: oberon.books@btinternet.com
www.oberonbooks.com

Tasso first published in this translation in 1994
by Oberon Books Ltd

A catalogue record for this book is available from the British
Library.

ISBN: 1 84002 162 4

Cover design: Andrzej Klimowski

Printed in Great Britain by Antony Rowe Ltd, Chippenham.

Contents

TASSO

Introduction

> 'My Iphigenie and Tasso were successful, because I was
> young enough to inform and enliven the idealistic material
> with my own sensuality. Now, at my age, such ideal subjects
> would not be suitable, and I would probably do better to
> choose material which already contains a measure of
> sensuality.'
>
> *Goethe at 80, in conversation with Eckermann,*
> *4 February 1829*

The composition of *Torquato Tasso* occupied Goethe from the
spring of 1780 until the summer of 1788, running through the
so-called 'classical' decade of his life, when he worked on
Iphigenie and the Helena episode of *Faust II*. In contrast to
those two works, though, the autobiographical content of *Tasso*
is not only exceptionally strong, but obviously so. The parallel
situations of hero and creator are inescapable: major poets in
the court service of benevolent and cultivated noblemen, both
engaged in love affairs of considerable ambiguity – Goethe's
relationship with Charlotte von Stein much resembles Tasso's
involvement with the Princess (only that Charlotte was not
relation to the Duke of Weimar, Goethe's employer). To
Eckerman Goethe admitted: 'The Court, the situation, the love
passages were at Weimar as at Ferrara.' Other parallels may be
less striking, though there are several possible models for the
remaining characters, and that of Antonio is clearly and
admittedly a reflection of Goethe himself in his position as
courtier and official in Weimar. The ambiguity – a word that
crops up all the time in dealing with this play – of the ending,
which continually vexes critical opinion, clearly shows Goethe's
indecision about which role he himself was playing; in Italy
he may have been Tasso, but in Weimar he was the Privy
Councillor. In this connection, it is worth mentioning the
possible influence of Goethe's friend from the 'storm and stress'
years, the writer Jakob Michael Reinhold Lenz, whose bizarre

appearance and conduct clearly called out the most Antonio-like qualities in Goethe himself. Lenz finally went insane from, among other things, disappointment with the failure of his ambitions, both artistic and social.

The first draft of *Tasso* was in what Goethe called 'poetic prose'; the composition foundered after two acts had been rapidly more or less finished. Five years later, in 1786, Goethe suddenly left for Italy, without a word of notice or farewell even to his closest friends: it is tempting to see here a parallel to Tasso's nervous collapse. Later, Goethe was to write: 'In respect of my fate I could compare myself to Tasso – the sorrowful momentum of a passionate soul drawn irresistibly towards exile is apparent throughout the whole work.'

The effect of Italy on Goethe was tremendous: he stayed there for two years, years he referred to as 'my rebirth'. When he returned to Weimar, his rebirth manifested itself pretty promptly in a considerable reorganisation of his way of life: the introduction into his household of Christiane Vulpius as his mistress estranged Frau von Stein, and their friendship was broken off. The end of *Tasso* had been overtaken by reality, and the ending of the play clearly lets a curtain fall on a period of the poet's life.

But it is finally the differences between people that are more interesting than the similarities, and one should beware of making a slick, simplistic judgment equating Goethe with Tasso, and leaving it at that. That Goethe was later exercised to play down the autobiographical element in the play is evident from the cut version he made for the first production (Weimar 1806). Unlike another possibly authorised stage version, the first Quarto of *Hamlet*, in which everyone's part is cut except the prince's, Goethe, removing some 800-odd lines, cuts more than twice as much from Tasso's part as from the rest of the parts put together.

The historical Torquato Tasso (1544–95) cannot nowadays claim many readers outside his own country, though his shorter poems, songs and madrigals are incomparable. His monumental epic *Jerusalem Delivered* strikes those strong-willed enough to persevere with it as being old-fashioned and unattractive in its central notions of religion, politics and society. As far as the play is concerned, it may be fortunate he is so widely unread: it would be a lot harder to write a play about Goethe, of whose genius and limitations we are assured, than about someone whose genius we must take on trust.

Tasso was born in Sorrento, the son of a poet, Bernardo, a relation and protege of the Duke of Salerno, whose pro-French sympathies he shared, sympathies for which they were expelled from Naples, fleeing first to Rome, then Urbino, at which court Tasso grew up. Tasso's mother stayed behind in Sorrento. After studying languages, law, philosophy and mathematics – a liberal education even for those days – he became famous on the publication of his epic *Rinaldo* in 1562: he was eighteen years old. In 1565 he joined the court of Cardinal d'Este, brother of Alfonso II, the ruling duke of Ferrara, whose court poet he became in 1571. Two years later he wrote his pastoral play *Aminta*, and in 1575 his masterpiece *La Gerusalemme Liberata*.

In the same year he took over the offices of court astronomer and historian from Antonio Montecatini, whose diplomatic success in Rome had earned him promotion to Chancellor. They were two men who should simply never have met; from so radical a clash of temperaments profound consequences were inevitable. Realism was bound to win, and Tasso's mental instability began to manifest itself about this time, further inflamed by a swing in critical opinion away from his work.

William Burroughs has said that 'a paranoiac is a man who's just found out what's going on'. Goethe's Tasso, surrounded by his four closest available friends, all of whom, in separate ways, have his welfare at heart, manages to misinterpret each of their interests in him, and to alienate them by the exercise of his affections for them, sulphurous in their possibilities, vitriolic in their effects. The Duke's patronage he interprets as exploitation, the Princess' platonic attachment as passion, Leonora's ambition as conspiracy, and Antonio's criticism as envy. Above all, *Tasso* is an examination of the paranoia which always affects, and often profoundly influences the creative artist, written by an artist who, as far as we can judge, was, like Richard Wagner, notably free of the complaint; this sign of health, however, indicates a certain lack of awareness of the way in which experience can be transmuted into art.

As his paranoia was fed by all those little indications we all save up until they seem 'proofs as strong as Holy Writ', the historical Tasso, subject to what psychiatrists call 'floating anxiety', became increasingly melancholic and irrational; he feared his servants were robbers and spies, that he was being denounced to the Inquisition, that fellow-courtiers were plotting his downfall. At one point he even demanded an investigation by the Inquisition, claiming to have serious doubts of the validity of certain fundamental beliefs. In the course of the investigation, a paranoid request if ever there was one, he managed, in case-book style, to implicate several other people, a dangerous precedent for a court whose position in relation to Rome made any religious irregularity a political statement.

Placed under a fairly benevolent surveillance, after trying to knife a servant he suspected of being a spy – for the Inquisition it need hardly be said – he nonetheless escaped in 1577 and fled to his sister in Sorrento. After a second abruptly initiated absence, he asked for permission to come back to Ferrara, but arrived during the preparations for the Duke's third marriage. Since no one had time to pay much mind to him, the ducal family in fact not receiving him, he fancied himself slighted and behaved accordingly. When someone becomes a problem, the solution is either to give him something, or take something away from him; in Tasso's case, the violence with which he expressed his resentment cost him his liberty. Governments uncertain about what to do with dissidents who are not actual criminals have always had one simple recourse to fall back on, and Tasso was thrown into an asylum where he stayed for seven years.

Incarceration badly affected his health, but the clarity and organisation of his writing during these years contradicts his accusers, or perhaps they congratulated themselves on having effected a cure. His fame grew, with successive editions of *Jerusalem* spreading his fame into Europe, and on his release in 1586 he found himself the most famous man in Italy – what dark suspicions this must have occasioned him we can only imagine. His last years were spent restlessly wandering from city to city, as if he was looking for the certainty, however grim, that prison had given him – rather like Oscar Wilde. In 1594 it was proposed to give him Italy's highest literary honour, already awarded to Petrarch and Ariosto, a crown of laurel leaves – compare the incident in the play – to be presented to him on the Capitol in the following spring. Unhappily, if typically, he died a few days before this could be done.

Surprisingly, Tasso's sensational life inspired only one dramatic predecessor to Goethe. Goldoni's *Il Tasso* (1755) was one of a trilogy of plays about writers, the other two being Molière and Terence. It has an offstage Duke, but makes up for it by having yet another Leonora, the Princess' maid, giving the hero a choice of three to be in love with: his choice of the Princess being discovered by the Duke – here her fiancée, not her brother – Tasso is incarcerated but finally released to go to Rome for his literary coronation. Much under-rated for its alleged trivialisation of the material, Goldoni's play is considerably superior in stagecraft to Goethe's. Equally autobiographical in content – how could such a theme fail to call out such feelings in a writer? – it replaces the romantic pathos of 'historical' cardboard Renaissance decor with the flippancy of the *ancien régime.* However, Goldoni, despite a fine scene in the asylum, where Tasso's seven-year stay is condensed into a single night, was unable, and would probably not have wished, to match the later poet's radical modernity of outlook that can still surprise us, although only a generation separates the two plays. It is hard to remember that Goldoni was still alive when Goethe's play was written: he seems as remote as Boccacio. It is this perhaps coincidental modernity that keeps the later play alive for a present-day audience. In an age of ambiguity, we easily identify with the uncertain. Heroes usually have, and certainly need some degree of vulgarity, but we do not always need heroes – only in emergencies.

Artists, like nations, have, and need, a strong side to enable them to cope with their neighbours and a weak side to enable their neighbours to cope with them. In Tasso's case, the strong side is his achievement, the weak side his character. Goethe's rather daunting remark, mentioned by Caroline Herder in a letter to her husband of March, 1789, that the subject of the play was 'the disproportion of talent to life' makes a lot more sense when we realise that it is not just the artist we are concerned with, and his inability to deal with the world, or the world with him, but with the fact that few of us are quite able to adjust to our social surroundings, and that it is our qualities of imagination, in other words the artist in all of us, that make it impossible for us to do so.

RDM
Vienna, 1990

Characters

ALFONSO II
Duke of Ferrara

PRINCESS LEONORA d'ESTE
his sister

LEONORA SANVITALE
Countess of Scandiano

TORQUATO TASSO

ANTONIO MONTECATINO
Secretary of State

The action takes place at Belriguardo,
the Duke's country estate.

A version of this translation was made for the Citizens' Company and was first performed by them at the Citizens' Theatre, Glasgow on 27 October 1982, with the following cast:

DUKE ALFONSO II, Peter Rumney

LEONORA D'ESTE, Kate Ingram

LEONORA SANVITALE, Jill Spurrier

TASSO, Dikran Tulaine

ANTONIO MONTECATINO, Ciaran Hinds
    with Colin Macneil, Stewart Porter

Producer, Robert David MacDonald

Designer, Michael Levine

A revised version was commissioned by the Actors Touring Company, and first performed by them on 2 October, 1990, with the following cast:

DUKE ALFONSO II, Peter Kenvyn

LEONORA D'ESTE, Madelina Nedeva

LEONORA SANVITALE, Helen Schlesinger

TASSO, Ian Hughes

ANTONIO MONTECATINO, Thomas Lockyer

Producer, Ceri Sherlock

Designer, Eryl Ellis

A further revision was first performed at the Lyceum Theatre, Edinburgh, on 15 July 1994, as part of the Edinburgh International Festival, with the following cast:

ALFONSO II, Andrew Wilde

LEONORE d'ESTE, Kathy Kiera Clarke

LEONORE SANVITALE, Irina Brook

TORQUATO TASSO, Henry Ian Cusick

ANTONIO MONTECATINO, Mark Lewis
    with Brendan Hooper, Stephen Wale

Director, Robert David MacDonald

Designer, Julian McGowan

Costumes, Hilary Baxter

ACT ONE

A garden, decorated with busts of the epic poets. Downstage, busts, to the right, of VIRGIL, to the left, of ARIOSTO.

PRINCESS: You watch me with amusement, Eleonora:
    yourself as well. What is it? Tell a friend.
    You look so thoughtful, although pleased enough.
LEONORA: To see the pair of us dressed up like this:
    rustic, ruder than Gothic, happy Dresden
    shepherdesses, even weaving garlands!
    Look at the colours, and the size of mine!
    You are much more high-minded, choosing laurel.
PRINCESS: I'm glad to say the wreath I wove in thought
    has found a worthy head already – Virgil.
    (*She crowns the bust of VIRGIL.*)
LEONORA: In which case Ariosto shall have mine:
    a share of the new spring for a genius
    who's like the spring itself.
    (*She crowns the bust of ARIOSTO.*)
PRINCESS: How kind it was,
    my brother's bringing us to Belriguardo
    so early in the year, where, by ourselves,
    the hours can pass as we dream back in time
    to the poets' golden age. I love this place:
    when I was young I spent such happy days here:
    the fresh green and the sunlight bring it back.
LEONORA: Yes, it's a brave new world, a brave new season.
    The trees, the fountains, soothe us and refresh us;
    young branches flutter, cradled on the breeze;
    the flowers in their beds gaze up like children;
    the gardener has opened up the orangery.
    The sky is blue and motionless above us,
    and on the mountains on the far horizon,
    the snow dissolves itself into a dew.
PRINCESS: I hate a spring that robs me of a friend.
LEONORA: Let us enjoy the time we have, and not
    remind each other how soon I must leave you.

PRINCESS: At least for you, the happiness you leave
    you'll find redoubled when you're back in Florence.
LEONORA: Duty and love both call me to my husband:
    he's been without me now for far too long.
    He needs to see his son, who's grown so much
    this year, and learned so much; I need to share
    in his paternal joy. But as for Florence,
    not all its wealth and treasure can compare
    to what you have here in Ferrara. People
    made Florence, princes made Ferrara great.
PRINCESS:
    Much more the brilliant men whom Chance brought here
    and genius and inclination kept here.
LEONORA: Chance can disperse as easily as she gathers.
    Great minds draw others to themselves, and know
    how to retain their loyalty, as you do.
    Your brother and you attract such people to you,
    proving yourselves your family's rightful heirs.
    When the Dark Ages still engulfed the world,
    the torch of learning was first kindled here.
    While I was still a child I'd heard the names
    of Ercole and Ippolito of Este.
    My father always spoke to me of Ferrara
    in the same breath as Rome and Florence. Petrarch
    was welcomed here, and Ariosto found
    his inspiration here. The whole of Europe
    can boast of few great names that have not been
    your guests. I longed to be, and now I am.
    There are advantages in giving genius
    one's hospitality: the gifts one gives
    will be repaid by gifts more priceless still.
    Genius sanctifies the ground it walks on.
    A hundred years from now his work will still
    be listened to by our great grandchildren.
PRINCESS: Only if they have your enthusiasm.
    Oh, how I envy you that!
LEONORA: But you feel things
    more clearly, more profoundly than the rest.
    I have to say whatever's in my heart,

but you can feel things deep down, and say nothing:
you are not blinded by appearances;
armed against wit, immune to flattery,
your mind stays firm, your taste impeccable,
your judgment sound. You have an eye for greatness
in others, recognising it in yourself.
PRINCESS: Close friendship's no excuse for flattery.
LEONORA: Close friendship is impartial: it is all
that values you for what you really are.
Even allowing for luck and opportunity,
the part they both played in your upbringing
is meaningless without the mind to work on,
and that you have, that finally is you.
And all the world admires you and your sister,
two of the greatest women of our time.
PRINCESS: That means so little, Leonora, when
I think how small one person is, how all
that person is, is owed to other people.
It was my mother taught me Greek and Latin
and appreciation of the ancient world.
But neither of her daughters ever could
have vied with her for quality of mind:
if either could, then it would be Lucretia.
Also, I promise you, I've never thought
my rank entitled me to gifts which were
the legacy of Nature, or pure chance.
I am all too relieved, when clever men
are talking, if I can follow what they say:
whether it's their opinion of some hero
of classical antiquity, and his deeds;
or the discussion of some branch of science,
which, by extension through experience,
will profit and improve Mankind. I'm happy
to follow, and to listen to whatever
they may discuss: the forces, which, both kind
and formidable, move the human heart;
the lust for fame, or power, or great possessions;
such subjects, treated by a clever man,
cease to be enigmas, and are made quite plain.

19

LEONORA: And after all that serious conversation,
    our ear and inner sense rest gratefully
    on poetry and music, which can mirror
    the deepest, finest feelings in our beings.
    Your mind is broad enough to cover continents,
    but mine prefers to wander round the island
    of poetry, the garden of the Muses.
PRINCESS: Despite there being nine of them, I am
    assured, they are less often in demand
    as playmates and companions than one might
    have thought: the artist is much more attractive,
    even if he does seem to avoid us,
    to fly from us indeed, apparently
    searching for something that's beyond our ken,
    and probably beyond his in the end.
    It would be nice though, if he were to stumble
    upon us by pure chance, and recognise
    with ill-concealed delight that we were what
    he had been vainly seeking through the world.
    A hit?
LEONORA: A touch, a touch, I do confess;
    the wound, however, is quite superficial.
    I judge men by their worth. I am not biased
    where Tasso is concerned. He hardly seems
    to see the world: the only thing he hears,
    the Harmony of Nature. All that Life,
    or History can offer him, he grasps
    greedily and at once; his temperament
    reconciles all their contradictions:
    his sensibility can give the spark of life
    to what was lifeless. What to us seems common
    he can ennoble, what we thought was fine
    he makes look worthless. And he draws us in
    to the enchanted circle he inhabits,
    to follow him, to take part in his journey.
    He seems to approach us, yet still keeps his distance;
    he looks at us, but strangely, just as if
    he saw straight through us, as if we were ghosts.

PRINCESS: A true and faithful portrait of The Poet,
    but I suspect reality attracts him
    as powerfully as dreams. The songs we find
    pinned on the trees from time to time, and which,
    like golden apples, recreate the garden
    of the Hesperides – do you not see
    in them the tangible, exquisite fruits
    of very real love?
LEONORA: I find them charming,
    like you. But all his work, however varied,
    is there to glorify a single figure.
    Sometimes he lifts her up among the stars,
    adoring her like an angel in the clouds;
    sometimes he follows her through quiet fields,
    weaving each flower he finds into a garland.
    If she eludes him, then the ground she trod
    is hallowed by her footsteps. In the thicket
    he hides, and like the nightingale, he fills
    the grove with musical complaint, poured out
    from a lovesick heart. His sadness is alluring,
    his song seductive, irresistible...
PRINCESS: And when he gives the object of this love
    a name, he chooses that of Leonora.
LEONORA: It is your name just as much as mine.
    I should resent it if he chose another.
    I'm happy in the ambiguity
    which masks his feelings for you: if our name
    reminds him of me too, I am delighted.
    There is no question here of love which seeks
    to master and possess exclusively
    the object of its passion, nor to guard it
    jealously from the sight of other people.
    He's not – I must say this, forgive me – he
    is not in love with us. He takes the things
    he loves from every sphere and part of life
    and gives a name to them that we both hear,
    sharing his feelings with us. So we seem
    to love the man, whereas in point of fact

> we needs must love the highest when we see it
> and he has shown it to us: we love that.

PRINCESS: Such deep philosophy calls all in doubt:
> I hear you but I hardly understand.

LEONORA: A student of Plato, and not understand
> what a mere novice says? I can't be wrong!
> Plato maintains Love's not a spoilt brat,
> but a god who has a powerful voice in council:
> not one that flits from one heart to another
> paying for his infatuations
> with disillusion and disgust, but forming
> firm, lasting bonds with character and beauty.

PRINCESS: Here is my brother. Do not mention where
> this conversation led to. It's enough
> our costumes having to endure his mockery
> without our having to do so as well.

DUKE: (*Entering.*)
> Have you seen Tasso? I can't find him anywhere.
> Not even here with you.

PRINCESS: I saw him yesterday
> just for a moment, not at all today.

DUKE: His usual fault, preferring solitude
> to our society. I would not mind his
> fleeing the madding crowd's ignoble strife
> if only he would not avoid his friends.
> Loneliness leads to nothing but ill-humour.

LEONORA: If I'm not much mistaken, Duke, you will
> soon see your criticism turn to praise.
> I saw him in the distance earlier,
> notebook in hand, writing, pacing, writing.
> He told me yesterday his work was finished
> or would be after 'just a few corrections',
> a final *coup de maître* before he laid it
> at the feet of the man to whom he owed so much.

DUKE: He shall be very welcome, *if* he brings it.
> We'll let him take a good long holiday.
> Much as I share in his work, much as I take
> considerable pleasure in it, as I must,

my patience is becoming rapidly
exhausted. He can never finish anything,
always half-ready, endless alterations:
one step forward, two steps back and then
another stop – our expectations cheated;
and most particularly so when we
are robbed of pleasure which we thought so near.
PRINCESS: Every great artist has a certain diffidence:
he takes such pains to fashion what he wants,
approaching step by step. You cannot turn
that much variety into harmony
in minutes: and his only interest
is how to round his work out to a whole.
He does not want a chain of fairy tales
which may be entertaining, but which will
leave one disappointed in the end.
Let him be, brother, works of art are not
judged by the time spent making them. If a man
is writing for posterity, then the world
of his contemporaries must stand aside.
DUKE: Let us join forces, sister, as we have
so often done before to great advantage.
If I'm impatient, teach me moderation,
and vice versa: in that way, perhaps,
we'll get him to his goal, as well as ours.
Ferrara, Italy, the world indeed,
can marvel at a finished masterpiece.
I shall have played my modest part in it,
and Tasso will be introduced to *Life*.
No genius can learn things in a vacuum:
it needs a world, a universe to train it.
An artist must learn to shoulder fame and blame,
be driven to impartial judgement of
himself, as well as others. Isolation
is a nursery which he must soon outgrow.
Enemies *won't* spare him, friends *must* not.
The boy must exercise his strength in combat,
learn what he is, and know himself a man.

LEONORA: Then you will still do everything for him,
    just as you have already done so much.
    A talent may be formed in solitude:
    but character needs the currents of the world.
    If only he could discipline his mind
    at your suggestion, as he does his art.
    If only he would stop avoiding people:
    suspicion turns to fear, and fear to hatred.
DUKE: You only fear what you cannot understand:
    you cannot understand what you avoid.
    You cannot master self-control in solitude,
    let alone control of other people.
    And that is Tasso's problem. I can see
    his mind becoming more and more confused,
    until his own thoughts take him prisoner.
    He worries more than is quite suitable
    about my favour, mistrusts everyone
    within a mile of him, who I am sure
    are in no way his enemies. If a letter
    goes astray, a servant gives his notice,
    a document is mislaid, immediately
    he smells intention, trickery, betrayal,
    and dark and devious plans to undermine him.
PRINCESS: But everyone must be to some extent
    the product of their own peculiarity:
    one can't divorce one's nature from oneself.
    If one's companion stubs his toe out walking,
    we should be glad to walk a little slower,
    and willingly extend our hand to him.
DUKE: I really think he ought to take a cure,
    on medical advice. Far better that,
    than try so hard to keep up with the healthy.
    My dears, I hope I'm not too rough a surgeon.
    I do my best, I represent security
    for him, I show considerable favour
    to him, in situations where such favours
    can be seen to be done. If he complains –
    what am I saying 'if'? – *when* he complains

I have investigations made at once,
as I did lately when he thought his rooms
were being searched. If nothing comes to light,
I try to make him see things as I see them:
and since there's nothing won't improve with practice,
I practice patience – and God knows I need it –
with Tasso. I am sure you both agree
he well deserves the effort. Now that I
have brought you here, I must get back to town
tonight. Antonio will be here from Rome
to fetch me: we have much to talk about,
decisions, letters, all of which demand
my going back this evening, I'm afraid.

PRINCESS: Shall we go back with you?

DUKE: No, no, stay here
at Belriguardo – go to Consandoli,
enjoy the weather while you can.

PRINCESS: But must you go?
Can you not organise things just as well
from here?

LEONORA: To rob us of Antonio
before he's told us all the news from Rome!

DUKE: Out of the question, children, but we shall
return as soon as may be, when you can
interrogate him at your leisure, and
help me to show my gratitude for all
his services on my behalf. Once we
have done our business, then perhaps we might
make up a party, and invite a crowd,
produce some animation in the gardens:
why, even I might feel myself entitled
to make an assignation in the glade.

LEONORA: We shall be happy to avert our gaze.

DUKE: You know how fearfully discreet I am.

PRINCESS: (*Looking off.*)
I have been watching Tasso for some time.
He's coming this way. No, he's not. He's stopped.
He's hesitating. No, he's really coming.

25

DUKE: Leave him to dream. He's like a sleepwalker
    when he is working, and one should not wake him.
LEONORA: No, he has seen us and is coming over.
TASSO: (*Entering with a parchment-bound volume.*)
    I hesitate to bring you this, and hardly
    can bring myself to part with it. I know
    it's still unfinished, even if it looks
    complete. My first concern was not to give
    it to you *in*complete, *now* I'm concerned
    at seeming *too* concerned, or too ungrateful.
    And as a man will throw himself upon
    the mercy of his friends, saying, 'Here I am,'
    so I say, 'Here it is': and please accept it.
DUKE: You overwhelm me. A red-letter day!
    At last I hold it in my hands, my work,
    as in a sense it is. I never thought
    I'd live to see the day when you'd at last
    decide to say 'It's finished. Here it is.'
TASSO: If you are satisfied, it is complete –
    since it is yours, in every sense. The work
    I put into it, the handwriting, are mine:
    but, looking closer, all that gives it value,
    I realise I have from you alone.
    If Nature chose to favour me with talent,
    Fortune perversely chose to treat me harshly.
    When I was young the beauty of the world
    attracted me, but all the time I had
    to think about our poverty at home.
    My parent's sufferings made every song
    I sang a dirge. You saved me from all that,
    freed me from deprivation, and removed
    the weight of worry from my shoulders, gave me
    not only freedom for my talent to develop,
    but also courage to allow it to.
    Whatever prize my work can win belongs
    to you alone, and I must thank you for it.
DUKE: Your modesty does you credit and us honour.
TASSO: If only I could tell you how aware
    I am that all this favour comes from you.

That inexperienced boy – could he have drawn
poetry from himself? Could he invent
the strategy of this war, the fighting skills
of heroes at the moment of decision?
How could I ever have described the wisdom
of the generals, the courage of the soldiers,
the battlefield of vigilance and cunning,
had not you, Prince, instilled all this in me,
as if you were my genius, taking pleasure
in demonstrating his supremacy –
his unattainable supremacy –
through the medium of some ordinary mortal.

PRINCESS: Then share our pleasure in your work.

DUKE: Enjoy
the applause of all good judges.

LEONORA: All the world!

TASSO: This moment is enough for me. All the time
I worked on it, my thoughts were all of you.
I aimed to please you, longed to entertain you.
For if we cannot make our friends our world,
we don't deserve the world should notice us.
Here is my country, this is where I find
I am at home. I listen here, I watch
minutely every gesture. Here I find
experience, knowledge, taste, I see two worlds,
that of the Now, and of Posterity.
Artists can lose their bearings in a crowd:
the only people we should listen to,
the only people who should judge or praise,
are those of understanding, like yourselves.

DUKE: If we represent the double world,
of Now and of Posterity, we cannot
merely accept your work, we must reward it.
(*Pointing to the bust of VIRGIL.*)
I see upon your mighty forbear's brow
the emblem of the artist. Was it chance,
or your good angel put it there? No matter.
I hear him say 'Why give the dead these honours?
The artist needs reward while he's alive.

If you still honour and admire us, then
give him the crown: green leaves belong to life.'
(*He beckons his sister, who takes the wreath from the bust and goes over to TASSO. He steps back.*)

LEONORA: You can't refuse. Look at the hand that offers it.

TASSO: Oh, let me hesitate: I cannot grasp
what will be left of life beyond this moment.

DUKE: Fame frightens you: you must learn to enjoy it.

PRINCESS: Tasso, would you deny me the rare pleasure
of silently expressing what I feel?

TASSO: Then I accept it, from your hands, although
I don't deserve it. Should I kneel?
(*The PRINCESS puts the wreath on his head.*)

LEONORA: (*Applauding.*)
Well done! Congratulations on the first of many.

DUKE: A foretaste of the crown the world will give you.

PRINCESS:
With loud applause. But friendship speaks more quietly.

TASSO: Take it away. It scorches like the sun.
It burns the power of thinking from my brain,
like fever. No, it is too much. Forgive me.

LEONORA: It gives protection in the tropic zones
of fame.

TASSO: Wreaths are for heroes. I do not
deserve refreshment or protection. No!
The gods should take it, place it in the clouds,
and always out of reach, so that my life
should be a constant pilgrimage to attain it.

DUKE: Early success can lead us to an early
appreciation of material things,
which, once enjoyed, we cannot do without,
and, once possessed, must be fiercely defended.

TASSO: And such defence must spring from inner strength
which will not fail us, as mine now fails me.
How soon good fortune saps the natural power
that fights adversity and braves injustice!
Has the delight, the rapture of the moment,
sucked out the very marrow of my bones?
Highness, I kneel down once again, to ask you,

ungraciously I know, take back your gift,
and let this all have been a dream from which
I've woken up to start my life afresh.
PRINCESS: But if you can accept the talent which
God gave you, can you not accept a gift
from us, however poor, the best we have?
Once you have worn the garland you can never
escape the mark of it upon your brow.
TASSO: Then I must go away in shame, and hide
my joy in the same dark wood where I
once hid my grief, and walk there, where no eye
reminds me of my undeserved good fortune.
And if the water's mirror ever shows me
the figure of a man bizarrely crowned,
against the sky, among the rocks and trees,
resting in contemplation, I shall think
it is Elysium, and ask myself:
just who might this departed spirit be?
A boy out of the past? So brightly crowned?
What is his name? Just what has he achieved?
And I shall think: if only there could be
others who'd come to join him, if the poets
and heroes of the ancient world would come
and meet together at the water's edge,
inseparable as they were in life!
Just as magnetic force draws steel to steel,
striving unites the hero and the poet.
Homer's whole life was dedicated to
the selfless contemplation of two men.
And Alexander, in the Elysian fields,
will run to seek out Homer and Achilles.
If only I could witness that reunion!
LEONORA: Wake up, wake up. You must not let us think
you cannot set a value on the present.
TASSO: It is the present that I value most:
if I seem absent-minded, it must be
your magic that has spirited me away.
PRINCESS: I'm glad to hear you converse with us spirits
so humanly.

(*A PAGE comes up to DUKE and silently hands him
something.*)

DUKE: Antonio? Show him in.
 And in good time. Ah, here he comes already.
 Welcome both to yourself and your good news.

PRINCESS: How good to see you!

ANTONIO: (*Entering.*) I can hardly tell you
 how much I missed you all. You seem contented
 with what I have achieved, reward enough
 for all that worry, all those tedious days,
 spent either in frustration, or in causing
 frustration to other people...such a waste.
 But we have what we wanted: no more quarrel.

LEONORA: You still have one with me, since you insist
 on arriving the moment that I have to leave.

ANTONIO: You rob my happiness of its completion
 by taking away the better part of it.

TASSO: May I say welcome too? I hope to profit
 from the company of a man of such experience.

ANTONIO: You'll find me quite reliable, if you deign
 to come down from Parnassus for a visit
 to my prosaic, albeit real world.

DUKE: You told me in your letters *what* you'd done,
 I'm curious still, though, about *how* you did it.
 Rome is a special case: one must be careful
 where, and on whom one treads to reach one's goal.
 To serve one's master's interests impartially
 is not an easy matter. Rome takes all
 and offers little in exchange. Go there
 with expectations – they'll be disappointed:
 go there with 'something', and you may be lucky.

ANTONIO: I used no arts and less negotiation.
 What politician has not met his match
 in the Vatican? Coincidence played right
 into our hands. His Holiness admires you –
 he sends his blessing, and recalls with pleasure
 the last time he embraced you. For your sake
 he did much.

DUKE: I'm delighted he has such
     a good opinion of me, insofar
     as it can be sincere. The Vatican
     looks down on emperors squabbling at its feet;
     how much more so on us lesser mortals?
     What was the factor which you found most useful?
ANTONIO: His Holiness is a pragmatic man.
     He sees the small as small, the great as great.
     To rule the world he is prepared to make
     concessions to his neighbours. He assesses
     the strip of land he cedes you at the value
     he puts upon your friendship. Italy
     needs peace, and he needs friends to keep it.
     Then he can lead united Christendom
     against the Infidel.
PRINCESS: Who are his friends?
     Is it known whom he trusts, whom he confides in?
ANTONIO: He listens only to experienced men,
     and only trusts hard-working ones. The servant,
     since childhood, of the state he now controls,
     his influence is felt in all those courts
     he knew as Nuncio many years ago,
     often shaping their policies even then.
     He sees the world as clearly as he sees
     his own advantage, and to see him working
     is to admire him, and find satisfaction
     when Time discovers what he has long prepared.
     There is no finer spectacle in the world
     than a prince who rules with wisdom, and an empire
     where all obey with pride, and all imagine
     they serve themselves alone, because the laws
     that they obey are just.
LEONORA: How I should love
     to see that world close to!
DUKE: And be part of it?
     You'd hardly be content to stay a mere
     observer; surely we'd want, from time to time,
     to stick our delicate fingers in the pie
     of power…no?

LEONORA: If you are trying to tease me,
    you won't succeed.
DUKE: We have old scores to settle.
LEONORA: Then one has just been settled. Now forgive me,
    and kindly do not interrupt my questions.
    (*To ANTONIO.*)
    What does he do to help his relatives?
ANTONIO: Neither more nor less than he ought to do.
    Even the people will despise a man
    in power who doesn't take care of his own.
    The Holy Father knows just how to use
    his family as good servants of the state,
    fulfilling two obligations at one blow.
TASSO: Does he encourage art, patronise learning –
    like the princes of the past?
ANTONIO: He honours learning
    where it will serve his purpose, help him rule
    a nation. As for art, he values it
    where it can decorate and glorify
    his capital, and help to make the city
    the wonder of the world. To be approved of
    everything has to serve a purpose. Everything
    must earn its keep. He is, as I said, pragmatic.
DUKE: How soon d'you think we can complete the business?
    Or will they put fresh obstacles in our path?
ANTONIO: Unless I'm very much mistaken, it
    will only need your signature and a letter
    or two to settle the quarrel once for all.
DUKE: Then this day indeed is a state-occasion:
    our frontiers extended and secured
    without the shedding of a drop of blood!
    We should present you with a civic crown.
    The girls shall weave you one, and we shall crown
    you with it in the morning. Meanwhile Tasso
    has brought his tribute too – his *magnum opus*
    is finished – yes, Jerusalem is conquered!
    His industry and courage have achieved
    his lofty, distant goal, and have thereby

put modern Christendom to shame, and so
we crowned him for his trouble.
ANTONIO: That explains
the riddle of the two crowned heads I saw
when I arrived – with some bewilderment,
if I may say so.
TASSO: But you only see
the outward, visible signs of my success.
I wish that, at the same time, you could see
the inward signs of shame.
ANTONIO: There are no bounds
to His Highness's generosity: you have just
found out what all of us have known for years.
PRINCESS: You'll find our praises just, and moderate,
when you see what he has achieved. We are
the first to applaud a masterpiece. The future
will only confirm our opinion ten times over.
ANTONIO: His reputation is secure with you.
If *you* value him so highly, who can argue?
But tell me, who was it crowned Ariosto?
LEONORA: I cannot tell a lie, it was this hand.
ANTONIO: Well done! It suits him better than the laurel.
In the same way as Nature uses greens
of various kinds to dress the world in, so
he uses various stories, seemingly
harmless or even trivial, to adorn
the things that make men loveable, or honourable.
Experience, understanding, strength of mind,
taste, and a sense of what is good and true,
his verse, and all his characters portray them.
Beauty is superfluity, and its source
flows alongside us, teeming with strange creatures:
the sky is filled with rare exotic birds,
forests and fields are filled with unknown beasts,
all dancing to the magic of his song.
Deceit may lurk half-hidden in the thickets,
but wisdom will from time to time descend
as noble music from a golden cloud.

33

Meanwhile his well-tuned instrument is able
to encompass even madness: all the time
the rule is moderation, and control.
The man who dares compare himself to him,
deserves a crown for sheer temerity.
Forgive me, I must seem a man possessed.
All these artists, all these wreaths, these dresses…
transport me to strange countries of the mind.

PRINCESS: If you can judge one genius so exactly,
you will have no difficulty with another.
You will show us qualities in Tasso's work
which we can only feel, things only you
can understand about it.

DUKE: Come along:
I still have much to ask you. After that
the ladies may have undisputed use
of you till sunset. Come along. Till later.
(*ANTONIO follows the DUKE, TASSO the ladies.*)

ACT TWO

TASSO: Princess, I follow you uncertainly.
   Thoughts with no proper order or proportion
   rise in my brain. The thought of solitude
   seduces me, and whispers in my ear:
   'I can resolve these newly-risen doubts.'
   Then I look at you, I hear you speak;
   a new day dawns, all fetters fall away.
   I willingly confess, Antonio's
   sudden arrival, unexpectedly,
   woke me up, none too softly, from a dream:
   his manner, what he said, affected me
   to such a degree, I feel myself once more
   divided and at war against myself.
PRINCESS:
   You cannot expect an old friend who's been absent
   for such a long time to pick up the threads
   exactly where he left them, the first moment
   he reappears. He won't have changed inside;
   you'll see, a few days living with him will
   tune the strings again, back to the harmony
   we're used to. He will realise more clearly
   just what you have achieved in these last months,
   and place you on a pedestal alongside
   the giant he tried to make your competition.
TASSO: Such praise of him, from him, amused me more
   than it insulted me. It's good to hear
   praise for a man in whom we recognise
   the master of us all. We tell ourselves
   if we achieve a fraction of his greatness
   we share a fraction of his honour. No,
   what struck me, while Antonio was speaking,
   was how the Pope, that uniquely clever man,
   controls the restless movement of those figures
   that populate that other world around him:
   I listened eagerly, with real pleasure,

to Antonio's assured, experienced words.
The more I heard, the more my spirits sank,
I felt myself like Echo, disappearing
into the rocks, a nothing, a reflection.
PRINCESS: And yet just now you seemed to be convinced
poets and heroes sought each other out,
lived for each other, neither showing envy.
The deeds that give a poet inspiration
are splendid, but the songs those deeds inspire
are every bit as splendid, don't forget.
Why not stay in the safety of Ferrara
and watch the currents of the world, in calm,
as if observing from the river bank?
TASSO: But it was here I first saw, with amazement,
how action is rewarded. When I came here,
young, orphaned, inexperienced, I gasped
to see the festivals, the tournaments,
which made Ferrara seem the centre of
the world. Oh, Heavens! What a sight it was!
Courage and skill shone in the open square
before a company the sun will not
shine on a second time. The fairest women,
the first men of our time, all crowded there.
My dazzled eyes took it all in, I thought:
'Has Italy, that narrow, sea-girt land,
sent them all here, to us? Why, this must be
the most illustrious court ever to sit
in judgment over honour, merit, virtue –
nobody here needs feel shame for his neighbour!'
And then the gates were all thrown open. Horses
pawed the ground and shields and helmets shone,
the grooms thronged in, the fanfares brayed, and lances
shattered, as shields and helmets struck and clanged,
and swirls of dust enveloped for a moment
the victor's glory and the loser's shame.
But I must let a curtain fall upon
that all too brilliant show: or I shall
feel my own lack of merit all too clearly.

PRINCESS: While you were being stirred to emulation,
    I could have given you a quiet lesson
    in patience. I never saw the festivals
    so many have described, both then and since.
    I lay in silence, where the fading echoes
    of pleasure died before they came to me.
    Lying in pain and filled with black depression,
    presentiments of death would come between
    me and the world, and only gradually
    did I begin to see the pale but welcome
    colours of life revive. The very day
    I left my sick-room, still supported by
    the nurses, there was my sister, all life and health,
    leading you by the hand. You were the first
    new face I saw on entering my new life.
    I hoped so much for you, and me: and so far,
    hope has not totally betrayed us, has it?
TASSO: And I, bewildered, dazzled by such splendour,
    prey to confused emotions, walked along
    beside your sister, through the silent palace,
    entering the room where you appeared
    supported by your ladies – oh, forgive me!
    Just as the presence of the god can cure
    a man bewitched, of all his mad illusions,
    so was I cured of all my false desires,
    all my fantasies, every wrong obsession,
    in that one moment when our glances crossed.
    My inexperience till then had made me
    waste my affections in the vain pursuit
    of a thousand objects: now, I could step back
    inside myself and learn, with shame, to know
    the nature and the worth of my ideal.
    It was as if I'd searched through every grain
    of sand of every ocean of the world
    to find a pearl, and found it in the end
    sleeping secure and hidden in its shell.
PRINCESS: Yes, that was the start of many happy days,
    and had my sister not been taken away

by the Duke of Urbino, then we could have passed
years of undistracted happiness.
We miss her, though, too much, her heart and mind,
so full of cheerfulness and courage,
her wit, her grace, and everything about her.
TASSO: I knew the day she left that you would find
no one who could replace her, and it broke
my heart. I used to ask myself
'Why is it only she that has the right
and happiness to mean so much to you?
Is there no other heart you can confide in?
Is there no other soul in tune with yours?
No other qualities of heart and mind?
Why should one woman, wonderful as she was,
be all?' Forgive me, Highness, if I thought
that sometimes to myself, wishing that I
could come in time to mean something to you:
little as it might be, it might be something.
I wished to show you, not with words, but actions,
how my whole life was secretly devoted
to you. But I could not: I made mistakes
that hurt you, I insulted those whom you
protected, clumsily confused what you
were trying to resolve. Each time I tried
to approach you, I felt more and more I was
a stranger.
PRINCESS: Tasso, I have never failed
to read your wishes in your mind. Too often
you are your own worst enemy. Unlike
my sister, who is at home with everyone,
you've hardly, even after all these years,
found anyone whom you can call a friend.
TASSO: All right, find fault with me, but only tell me
where do I find a man, or woman, whom
I could confide in as I do in you?
PRINCESS:
You should have much more confidence in my brother.
TASSO: He is my master – but you must not think
I harbour any wild desire for Freedom.

Mankind was not created to be free;
the best activity of a noble mind
is happily to serve a prince he honours.
Well, then, your brother is my prince. I fully
realise the implications of the word.
I must learn to be silent when he speaks,
obey when he gives orders, even if
my head and heart both flatly contradict him.
PRINCESS: That's not a very likely thing to happen:
not with my brother. And now we have Antonio
among us once again: there is a new
and talented companion.
TASSO: So I hoped
at first, but now I have my doubts. I could
profit both from his company and advice.
I see he has every quality I lack.
But even if all the gods were present at
his christening and showered him with gifts,
the Muses were conspicuous by their absence:
and anyone they fail to favour may
possess a great deal, give a great deal, but
provides no comfort.
PRINCESS: But he can be trusted.
And that is much. You must not look for all
in one man, and this one delivers what
he promises, a man to be relied on.
Once he has said he is your friend, he will
do everything to give you what you lack.
You must be friends with him. I flatter myself
I know the right way to arrange it, quickly.
Just don't put up your customary resistance.
Yes, customary, look at Leonora...
elegant, beautiful, kind, accessible,
she's been with us for months, and still you've never
once approached her as she would have liked.
TASSO: I have done what you wanted, I have not
avoided her, which would have been my instinct.
However kind she seems – I don't know why

it is – I never could be open with her.
If she contrives to help a friend, you always
sense the contrivance...that spoils everything.

PRINCESS:
That's not a road on which you'll find much company.
Tasso, that way will lead you into quicksands
and jungles, where your nature will become
increasingly turned in upon itself,
and self-indulgently strive to restore
within itself the Golden Age, of which
it feels such desperate lack outside itself,
however fruitless such an enterprise.

TASSO: Your Highness takes the words out of my mouth.
'The Golden Age.' Where has it vanished to?
The age the whole world longs for, and in vain?
When men could walk the earth as free as beasts,
shepherds and shepherdesses sat beneath
the shade of ancient trees, while tenderer boughs
grew closely round the flowering of love;
the river, clear and still upon a bed
of virgin sand, cradled a nymph, and in
the grass the startled snake would slide
harmlessly away: the deer, too bold,
swiftly evaded the young hunter's arrow;
and birds and beasts could speak to men and say:
'Do what thou wilt shall be the whole of the law.'

PRINCESS: My dear, the Golden Age is dead and gone:
only idealists are fool enough
to think they can revive it. And to tell
the truth, I think the golden age the poets
inflict on us was every bit as far
from them as it is from us. And even if
it did exist, it is no more than we
can recreate in our imaginations.
Kindred spirits can still meet to share
the beauties of the world. The only thing
that's different is the motto, which now reads:
'Do what thou wilt, provided it *is* the law'.

40

TASSO: If only all the wise men would decide
    what *is* the law: instead of everyone
    imagining that what suits him is right.
    The world is full of clever, powerful men
    doing just what they want, and making it
    the absolute standard of propriety.
PRINCESS: Ah, if you want to know about propriety,
    ask women of good family. They're the ones
    who have to take most care about propriety.
    Propriety surrounds us like a moat:
    and where there is propriety, we rule,
    and where there is vulgarity and insolence we're nothing.
    Put the question to both sexes:
    men may seek freedom, women seek propriety.
TASSO: You think all men unfeeling, coarse, insensitive?
PRINCESS: No. But their aims are higher, and their patience
    less, which means they must resort to violence.
    Men aim their actions at Eternity,
    where women only want a small estate,
    but want to know that it will last their time.
    We can't rely on any man's affection,
    however bravely it may burn to start with;
    since Beauty is the only thing you worship,
    and when that's gone, what's left no longer charms,
    and what no longer charms might just as well
    be gone along with all the rest. If men
    could just know how to esteem a woman's heart,
    and realise what fidelity and love
    a woman's breast could hold; if men could just
    retain the memory of happiness;
    if they could see through illness and old age
    as sharply as they see through everything else;
    if their possessions could bring peace, instead
    of merely tickling their appetite
    for further conquests: if there were men like that
    then we could talk about a Golden Age.
TASSO: What you just said reminded me of something
    I thought I had forgotten.

PRINCESS: What was that?
    What do you mean? Tasso, speak freely to me.
TASSO: I've often heard – and lately heard again –
    and if I hadn't heard I would assume –
    princes are asking for your hand in marriage.
    Of course, we must expect it; all the same
    we fear it, desperately. Oh, I know
    you will be leaving us, that's natural:
    but how we are to bear it...I don't know.
PRINCESS: There is no need to fear – not for the moment:
    I almost might say, not for ever. I...
    am happy here, and I should like to stay here.
    Nor can I think of any circumstance
    that could tempt me away: but if you wish
    to keep me here, then show me you can try
    to live in peace with everyone.
TASSO: I shall,
    if you will teach me how. The only time
    when I am truly happy is when I
    can shew my gratitude and dedication
    in what I write – and that is all for you.
    The goddesses of Earth are set above us,
    just as a higher destiny is set
    above the wills and minds of even the wisest.
    Goddesses stand aloof, and what we see
    as waves, are only puddles at their feet.
    They do not hear the tempests which destroy us.
    Our cries can scarcely reach them, and they let
    the air be filled with them, as we would let
    ignorant, wretched children cry, alone.
    You've been so patient with me, for so long.
    Your eyes have dried the dew that lay on mine.
PRINCESS:
    Women will always be your friends, and rightly,
    since what you write does so much honour to them.
    Gentle or brave, you know how to present them
    both nobly and attractively – and when
    Armida seems most hateful, we are soon
    reconciled by her beauty and her love.

TASSO: But everything I write I owe to one –
    one single source. The archetype of beauty;
    and what I draw from that must last for ever.
    The heroic love of Tancred and Clorinda,
    the silent, unseen loyalty of Erminia,
    Sophronia's greatness, and Olinda's pain.
    They are not shadows. My characters are not
    figments of my imagination, they exist.
    For ever. Nothing has more right to last
    for centuries than a secret declaration
    of love entrusted to the care of art.

PRINCESS: Then let me tell you of another virtue
    your poetry surreptitiously conveys.
    It forces us to listen over and over:
    we listen and we think we understand:
    and since to understand is to forgive,
    you see, you are the winner in the end.

TASSO: Oh, Princess, you have shown me Paradise,
    and, if the splendour of it does not blind me,
    I'll see a happiness I'd not dared hope for
    descend on me, eternal, radiant, golden.

PRINCESS: Tasso, no more. There are a lot of things
    which can and must be gained by force, while others
    yield only to self-denial, renunciation.
    They say that love and virtue are among them.
    They are related. Think about it. Carefully.
    (*She leaves.*)

TASSO: May I look up? Dare I look round? Alone.
    Or did these pillars hear the words she spoke?
    Must I fear witnesses, dumb witnesses,
    of a happiness surpassing all I dreamt of?
    The sun has risen on another life,
    surpassing everything that went before.
    The goddess has come down to raise me up,
    and a new world reveals itself to me!
    How utterly our prayers are sometimes answered!
    A blind man may form some idea of light
    and colour, but if they appear to him,

it is as a new sense. I'm still afraid,
but drunk enough with happiness to be
able to set my feet upon this path.
You give so much, as generously as Nature,
and in return you ask of me such things
as only givers of such gifts could dare.
Renunciation, self-denial – are these
what I must exercise to earn her trust?
What did I ever do that she should choose me?
What must I do to make me worthy of her?
She trusted me, and so I must be worthy.
Oh God, let her ask anything of me,
my life belongs to her: she may transform me
into whatever form she wishes, and
possess me utterly, while all my heart
possesses shall be held in trust for her.
A thousand talents would not be enough
to express those things that cannot be expressed.
I need no longer walk alone, indifferent
to men and trees, irresolute, depressed.
I cannot be alone, I am with her:
even her absence is a gift to me.
If only I could prove myself in action,
expose myself to danger, sacrifice
the life she's given me, I would – oh, gladly!
Why was I so rash as to reveal
my feelings far too soon, before I could
make myself worthy to show them? Well, it's done:
far better to receive such gifts unmerited,
unsought, than half presume one has the right
to make demands, and bargain over merit.
What lies before me is so great, so vast!
Youth and hope pull me on towards a future
radiant, unexplored. I am a tree
spreading a thousand branches to the sun,
unfolding into flower, ripening,
fruit disclosing, crop of sweetness, heavy,
waiting for her soft hand to take my harvest.

(*Enter ANTONIO.*)
This almost seems like our first meeting. Welcome:
no man more so, to me. I offer you
my hand and heart without reserve, and hope
you won't reject them.

ANTONIO: You are generous:
and if I hesitate before accepting,
it is because I recognise the value
of what you offer me, and am not sure
if I can quite reciprocate in kind.
And since I do not care to be exposed
to accusations of ingratitude
or over-hastiness, let me display
caution and discretion for us both.

TASSO: Who can blame you? Every step we take
betrays the need for moderation: but
it's better when our souls can tell us when
we have no need for caution.

ANTONIO: Everyone
should ask himself that question, since he must
live with the consequences of his own mistakes,
and weaknesses.

TASSO: Well, I have done my duty:
the Princess wished to have us friends again –
I have obeyed her, introduced myself.
I did not dare refuse, Antonio,
but rest assured I shan't impose on you.
Time and acquaintance may perhaps persuade you
to accept my friendship, which you set aside
so coldly now.

ANTONIO: The moderate man is often
thought cold by people who believe themselves
warm-hearted when they're merely over-heated.

TASSO: That is the fault I both hate – *and* avoid.
I'm not so young I don't know how to value
stability over passion.

ANTONIO: Very wise.
Let's hope you will remain of that opinion.

45

TASSO: You've every right to lecture me: you have
    experience behind you. But believe me,
    the silent heart hears promptings every minute
    which secretly impel it to pursue
    the Good which you imagine I had never
    known to exist until you chose to inform me.
ANTONIO: How nice it must be to be self-absorbed:
    and such a pity it is not more useful.
    Nobody learns to know himself by always
    looking inwards, measuring everything
    with his own yardstick: sometimes it's too short,
    more often much too long, unhappily.
    Men only recognise themselves in other men;
    only Life tells us what we truly are.
TASSO: I must agree with every word you say.
ANTONIO: And yet you put another meaning on
    my words, quite different from the one I meant.
TASSO: This is no way to reach an understanding.
    I cannot see that it is wise, or useful,
    deliberately to misunderstand
    a fellow-creature, be he who he may.
    I did not need Her Highness's suggestion –
    I know you want, and work for what is good,
    I know you seek for nothing for yourself,
    I know how loyally you support your friends.
    What sort of person would I be, if I
    did not admire that? if I did not try
    to emulate you in what ways I could?
    to seek a portion of that buried treasure
    you hide inside you? If you could be open
    you'd not regret it – if you only knew me,
    you'd be my friend. Why should I be ashamed
    of youth and inexperience? All the future
    still lies ahead of me. A friend like you
    I have long stood in need of. Oh, Antonio,
    take me and teach my inexperience
    and hastiness the uses of this world.
ANTONIO: You ask for something only Time can bring.

TASSO: Love, in a second, can achieve what time
and trouble scarcely bring about in years.
I do not ask this from you, I demand it –
in the name of that ideal that seeks to unite
good men – and shall I say another name?
The Princess wishes it – let us be friends.
Once more, here is my hand. Do not reject it.
Give me the pleasure which the noblest natures
must feel when they defer to one still nobler.

ANTONIO:
You've hoisted too much sail. You seem too used
to easy victories, and open doors.
I envy neither your talent nor your luck:
but I see all too clearly just how wide
and deep the gulf is that is fixed between us.

TASSO: In years, perhaps, not in determination.

ANTONIO: Deeds need not follow on determination:
courage sees every way as short: whoever
can reach a goal will get a crown, and some
will be deprived of crowns who more deserve them.
Still, there are garlands that are easily won,
garlands of many different kinds, God knows,
some to be won in the course of a morning's walk.

TASSO: Some things cannot be had just for the asking,
nor just for the desire: only the Gods
bestow them...or in some cases, withhold them.

ANTONIO: Put it down more to Fortune than 'the Gods',
since she is blind.

TASSO: Justice is blindfold too,
to avoid being dazzled by imposters.

ANTONIO: The ones whom Fortune favours, favour her:
but, of course, they think she has a hundred eyes,
all on the look-out for the slightest merit,
and sparkling with judgement and good taste.
A passing gesture seems a just reward,
and trinkets gained by chance due recognition.

TASSO: You need not make your meaning any clearer.
It is enough. I see into your heart.

I know you for a lifetime. Would her Highness
knew you so well! You need not waste your venom:
this garland on my head is proof against it.
And you can start by being man enough
not to begrudge me it, and then maybe
you might be worthy to compete with me
for what I see as my most dear possession.
Show me the man who can achieve one-tenth
of what I aim at, just show me the man
who has deserved it more, or blushes deeper
than I to have achieved it, and I shall
kneel to the Deity who gave it me
and beg that it be given to my rival.

ANTONIO: Until such time, you wear it winningly.

TASSO: While I can hardly silence criticism –
nor would I wish to – I have not deserved
contempt. The crown the Princess made for me,
the crown the Prince considered I deserved,
is not to be called in doubt with stupid jokes.

ANTONIO: I'd ask you to remember where you are,
and moderate your tone to me, if possible.

TASSO: What you permit yourself, I also may.
Or has the Truth been exiled? Is free thought
imprisoned in the palace? Can we only
expect oppression here? I must suppose
nobility – nobility of spirit –
here finds its proper sphere, and is that not
permitted to have contact with the great?
It may and shall. We may be intimate
with princes by the virtue of our birth;
why not as much by virtue of those gifts
which Nature gives as sparingly? Nobility
of spirit is as rare as pedigrees.
The only thing that needs to fear this place,
is pettiness, the only thing that needs
to be ashamed to show itself, is Envy! –
like spiders spinning dirty little webs
to foul these rooms.

ANTONIO: You show me just how right
 I am to hold you in contempt. A headstrong boy
 would like to force a man to be his friend,
 and trust him, would he? Tell me, do you think
 it does you credit to be so ill-mannered?

TASSO: More credit to be what you call ill-mannered,
 than to be what I would call despicable.

ANTONIO: Well, you're still young enough, and discipline
 may not arrive too late to teach you better.

TASSO: Old enough not to bow before false gods,
 and not too young to stand up for myself.

ANTONIO:
 Where voice and verse are what decide the issue,
 you doubtless come a hero from the field.

TASSO: I'd be a fool to boast about my strength,
 since I've not had to prove it – but I trust it.

ANTONIO: What you trust in is other men's protection,
 which has indulged your insolence far too long.

TASSO: I suddenly realise I am a man.
 I had no wish in the world to challenge you –
 but you heap fire on fire, until revenge
 becomes a physical necessity.
 If, therefore, you are a fraction of the man
 you boast of being…give me satisfaction.

ANTONIO: You forget both yourself, and where you are.

TASSO: No sanctuary compels me to stand here
 and be insulted. You defiled this place:
 you are profaning it, not I. I offered trust,
 love, admiration. It is you pollutes
 this Paradise, your words pollute this room,
 and not the feelings of my heart, which rise
 and overflow to wipe the stain away.

ANTONIO: Such mighty feelings in so small a breast.

TASSO: Still room enough to air those feelings in.

ANTONIO: Boasting to give you courage? Like a peasant.

TASSO: If you are a gentleman, then show it.

ANTONIO: I am indeed, and I know where I am.

TASSO: Then come outside, and find a place to fight.

ANTONIO: I shall not. You've no right to challenge me.

TASSO: Cowards will always welcome such restrictions.

ANTONIO: Cowards will only threaten when they're safe.

TASSO: Then happily I need no such protection.

ANTONIO: What you bring on yourself is unimportant.
    The court, however, is another matter.

TASSO: May it forgive your insults and my suffering
    them for so long.
    (*Draws his sword.*)
                Now draw or follow me –
    unless I am henceforth to hold you in
    contempt as everlasting as my hatred.

DUKE: (*Entering.*) Must I assume I interrupt a quarrel?

ANTONIO: Your Highness will discover I have kept
    my temper, under pressure from a madman.

TASSO: My lord, your glance subdues me, as I'd wish.

DUKE: Tell me, Antonio, both of you, how did
    this dispute force its way into my house?
    What has come over you? Dragged you from the path
    of manners, and good sense? I am astonished.

TASSO: This man, with all his reputation for
    diplomacy and wisdom, has behaved
    like an ill-bred, uneducated peasant.
    I came to him in trust, and he repulsed me:
    still I persisted, but he would not rest
    till he had turned the last drop of my blood
    to gall. Forgive me! You have found me here
    behaving like a madman. But this man
    should bear the blame if blame there is: he fanned
    the flames that seized on me and hurt us both.

ANTONIO: Make some allowance for poetic licence.
    But since you first addressed yourself to me,
    perhaps I may now be allowed to answer
    now that this fiery orator has done?

TASSO: Oh, yes, of course, tell all, tell every word.
    And if you can, repeat each syllable,
    each gesture. Let him judge. Accuse yourself.
    I'll not deny a single breath or heartbeat.

ANTONIO: If you have more to say, then kindly say it:
    if not, be good enough to hold your tongue,
    and do not interrupt. Your Highness asks
    whether this boy or I began the quarrel?
    And who was in the wrong? That is, of course,
    a larger question which I feel we needn't
    investigate too closely just at present.

TASSO: Why ever not? It seems to me the most
    important question – who was right or wrong.

ANTONIO: A mind unused to discipline might think so.

DUKE: Antonio!

ANTONIO: Your Highness's point is taken.
    But let him be silent until I have finished:
    then he may say his piece – you shall decide.
    My problem is, I cannot go to law
    against him, cannot sue him nor defend
    myself – nor can I give him satisfaction –
    because he is no longer a free man,
    having already broken the law which you,
    Your Grace, can only mitigate, at best.
    He threatened me and challenged me in this room,
    he scarcely troubled to hide his sword from you –
    had you not interposed yourself between us,
    I too might have been guilty of forgetting
    my duty.

DUKE: (*To TASSO.*) Then the fault was on your side.

TASSO: My lord, I think your heart will second mine
    in freeing me from guilt. Yes, it is true
    I threatened him, I challenged him, I drew on him:
    but you cannot conceive the spite, the malice,
    the calculated venom which his tongue
    injected in my veins, or how he fed
    the fire of my resentment – goading me,
    calm and controlled, provoking me to fury.
    You do not know him, and you never will.
    He threw my proffered friendship in my face,
    and I should be eternally unworthy
    of your respect if I had not reacted.

If I have overstepped the law, forgive me.
But I am neither vile, nor mean, nor base,
nor will I be reviled, demeaned, debased.
And if my heart at any time betrays you,
then punish me, reject me, banish me.
ANTONIO: How easily the boy can bear his burdens,
and shake his fault off, like dust from his clothes!
It really would be quite remarkable,
if poetry were not so celebrated
for being, unlike politics, the art
of the *Im*possible. Whether you, my Lord,
or those that serve you, can regard this matter
as trivial and unimportant, I
take leave to doubt. Authority protects
those who regard it as a shield and refuge,
and check their passions on approaching it.
It sheathes all swords and forces threats to silence;
anger and insult must find other fields
in which they can resolve their differences.
Here no traitor sneers, no coward flinches.
Your ancestors built a wall of safety here,
a sanctuary of human dignity,
keeping the peace by heavy penalties,
prison, exile and death fell on the guilty.
Compassion did not stay the hand of Justice,
nor did respect of persons: it was felt
as a deterrent, even by criminals.
But now, after a long peace, we can see
it's Law and Order that are threatened here
by a return to violence, which Your Grace
must punish, for, if neither Throne nor Law
can give protection, who can still do his duty?
Better some slight injustice than disorder.
DUKE: Impartial justice sees beyond what both
of you have said. That I must judge at all
would indicate you both failed in your duty.
But right and wrong are neck-and-neck in this,
and, if Antonio has insulted you,

then he must make amends, as you require:
I should be glad to be your referee.
Meanwhile, however, Tasso, your behaviour
requires me to arrest you. Since I pardon you,
I shall relax the law on your account.
Leave us. You are confined to your apartments:
on your assurance, both your prisoner
and guard.

TASSO: Is that your final sentence, Prince?

ANTONIO: Can you not see it as a father's mercy?

TASSO: I have no more to say to you. Your Grace
has ordered my imprisonment. So be it.
You have the right, and I obey your order,
enjoining silence on my inmost heart.
This is so new to me, I hardly know
myself or you or this place. Yet it seems
I am regarded as a criminal,
and certainly a prisoner – of conscience?
Whatever my heart may say, I am captive.

DUKE: You take this much more seriously than I do.

TASSO: I find it all incomprehensible –
perhaps not that – I'm not a child – just when
I think I see the point, it vanishes.
I only hear my sentence, and accept it.
Too many pointless words have passed already.
From now on I must get used to obedience:
how stupid of me to forget my place.
The kingdom of the gods seemed fixed on earth,
and now I am caught up in its dreadful fall.
Here is my sword, the one you gave me when
I went to France with the Cardinal. I won
no fame with it, but equally no shame,
not even today.

DUKE: Can you not understand
I am your friend? This is for your own good.

TASSO: I must obey you, Sir, not understand.
I must give back your other gifts as well.
Crowns never look quite right on prisoners.

Mine came to me too early, and it's now
taken away, a punishment for pride.
I was a king before I was a prince.
So take from me what none could take from you,
and what no god could give a second time.
What trials we are forced to undergo!
We'd never bear them if we had not been
gifted by Nature with inconsistency:
necessity drives us on to gamble, coolly
and recklessly with our most prized possessions.
We willingly let slip through our fingers
things we can never hope to have again.
So, there's a kiss – combine it with a tear
and consecrate it to oblivion.
Who would not weep when immortality
itself is not safe from destruction?
There. Join the sword with which I – did not win you:
lie there: it looks more like a cenotaph,
than the grave of my poor hopes and happiness.
There they both are, laid willingly at your feet.
If you are angry, what use is a weapon?
If you reject me, what use is a crown?
The prisoner goes now, to await his sentence.
(*DUKE signs to a PAGE, who picks up the sword and the
laurel wreath, and carries them off after TASSO.*)
ANTONIO: The boy's a lunatic. Where is he going?
A highly-coloured view of his own importance.
Youth in its inexperience always thinks
itself uniquely privileged to run
from one excess to another, with impunity.
He feels he's being victimised: although
he'll thank us for it, if ever he grows up.
DUKE: I fear the punishment may have been too harsh.
ANTONIO:
Prince, if you feel you should have been more lenient,
release him now, and we can fight our duel.
DUKE: If that is your opinion, I well may.
But tell me, how did you arouse his anger?

ANTONIO: I hardly know. I certainly did not
    insult him as a gentleman: however,
    I may have stung his *amour-propre* a little,
    though I admit that, even at his angriest,
    no untoward expression passed his lips.
DUKE: So I supposed. What you say now confirms
    my first impressions. When men disagree,
    the wiser is the guiltier. It would have
    looked better if you had tried to persuade him.
    Still, there is time: and there's no need to take
    the business any further. Just so long
    as I have peace, I'd like to keep him here.
    Make peace with him: you'll have no difficulty.
    Leonora Sanvitale might
    usefully use her arts to pacify him:
    then you restore his freedom in my name,
    and win his trust with frankness and nobility.
    Talk to him like a father and a friend.
    I want it done before we leave tonight.
    There's nothing you can't manage if you choose.
    Best we delay our journey for an hour,
    and leave the women to complete the work
    begun by you: and by the time we're back,
    they'll have removed all traces of this pother.
    It seems you can't resist keeping your hand in.
    One diplomatic business scarce completed,
    you come back here and make yourself another.
    I hope you have as much success with this one.
ANTONIO:
    What you say shows me I was wrong, more clearly
    than any mirror. Obedience is easy
    where masters can persuade where they command.

ACT THREE

PRINCESS: Where is Eleonora? Every moment
    weighs heavier on my heart. I hardly know
    what happened, which of them was in the right.
    If only she would come! I'd rather not
    speak to my brother yet, nor to Antonio,
    until I'm calmer, when I understand
    just how things stand, and what will come of it.
    (*Enter LEONORA.*)
    Tell me, how is it with our friend? What happened?
LEONORA: I can find out no more than we know already.
    They quarrelled. Tasso drew. Your brother parted them:
    only it would appear Tasso began it.
    Antonio is walking round quite freely,
    talking to Alfonso: on the other hand,
    Tasso's alone, confined to his apartments.
PRINCESS: Clearly Antonio irritated him:
    that cold aloofness must have hurt his feelings.
LEONORA: I think so too. A cloud was on his brow
    when we first saw him earlier this morning.
PRINCESS: Oh, we ignore the promptings of our hearts.
    A god speaks in us with a still, small voice,
    telling us what to grasp and what to shun.
    Antonio seemed withdrawn, abrupt, this morning,
    more so than usual. As they stood together,
    I had a premonition. Look at them!
    Their eyes, their faces, voices, even their walk –
    everything is at loggerheads. They cannot
    ever be friends. But Pharisaic hope
    deceived me into thinking: here we have
    two reasonable, educated men,
    both friends of ours, and what affinity
    is more elective? I persuaded Tasso
    and he agreed, so gratefully, so warmly.
    If only I had spoken to Antonio
    at once. There was so little time. I was

reluctant to begin the conversation
by mentioning Tasso: I relied on manners
and etiquette, the social code which is
so easy to observe, even with enemies.
I never dreamed Antonio could be capable
of letting passion rule experience.
I meant no harm, but through me harm is done.
What shall I do?

LEONORA: You surely see how hard
it is to give advice. We are not dealing
with a falling-out of men who think alike
where words, or swords, at worst, will end the matter.
I realised long ago these are two men,
whose mutual enmity is the result
of Nature's failure to make one man
of them instead of two. If only each
would see his own advantage, they'd unite
as friends and go through life successful,
happy, strong, as one man, as they say.
That's what I hoped – in vain, as things turned out.
This morning's quarrel, whatever it may have been,
will be smoothed over, but that gives us no
assurance for the future, even tomorrow.
How would it be, I wonder, if he were
to leave here for a while: and go to Rome,
or Florence for that matter? I could meet him
there in a week or two, and work on him,
as a friend, of course, and meanwhile you could work
upon Antonio, who almost seems
a stranger now. You must regain his friendship.
Time may work what seems otherwise impossible.

PRINCESS: While you enjoy the pleasure of the company
which I must do without. Now, is that fair?

LEONORA: What you will do without is only something
you cannot at the moment have in any case.

PRINCESS: Am I so calmly to exile a friend?

LEONORA: His exile will be in appearance only.

PRINCESS: My brother will be loth to let him go.

LEONORA: When he sees things as we do, he'll agree.
PRINCESS: Punishing friends is punishing oneself.
LEONORA: But if you save your friend, you save yourself.
PRINCESS: I cannot say yes unconditionally.
LEONORA: You're shoring up worse trouble for yourself.
PRINCESS:
    Don't torture me, you can't be sure you're right.
LEONORA: We'll soon discover which of us is wrong.
PRINCESS: Perhaps – don't talk about it any more.
LEONORA: Those who can make decisions conquer pain.
PRINCESS: Well, I've made no decision – yet – except
    to say he should not be away too long.
    Let us take care for him, though, Leonora,
    and see he wants for nothing in the future.
    My brother must continue to support him
    even when he's away. Talk to Antonio:
    he can persuade Alfonso, and will not
    bear grudges against Tasso or ourselves.
LEONORA:
    A word from you would help a great deal more.
PRINCESS: I am no good at begging favours for
    myself, unlike my sister. Once I used
    to wish I could: now I'm resigned to it.
    My friends still nag me: 'Oh, you're so unselfish!
    All very well,' they say, 'but you're so much so,
    you cannot feel the needs of those you love.'
    Having to cope with such reproaches, now
    I'm all the happier I can really be
    some help to a friend: and I can use
    the money from my mother's legacy.
LEONORA: Tasso's a child where money is concerned:
    but I can tell him how to manage it.
PRINCESS: Take him away then; if I must do without him,
    rather with you than anybody else.
    I see this is the best way to arrange things.
    And I must once more get into the habit
    of seeing suffering as medicine – 'good for one'.
    I should be used to it by now: I've heard

it ever since I was a child. It's easier
to bear the loss of happiness if we
have never counted on it in the first place.
LEONORA: I hope you will be happy – you deserve it.
PRINCESS: Happy, Eleonora? Who is happy?
My brother, I suppose, has got the courage
to face things, but he's had his disappointments.
My sister in Urbino? Beautiful,
and rich, and noble, and she cannot give
her somewhat younger husband any children.
He worships her and never blames her for it,
but still their house is wretched. And what help
was all our mother's cleverness? Did that
save her from heresy? They took us away
from her and now she's dead, and we cannot
even be sure she died at peace with God.
LEONORA: Do not think of the things that people lack.
Look what they *have!* Look what you have yourself!
PRINCESS: Patience, for one thing – painfully acquired
in childhood; I've had time to practice it.
When all the other children would be playing,
I would be lying there, an invalid,
a prisoner in my room. I had to learn
renunciation early. The one thing
that compensated for my loneliness
was music – I could entertain myself,
and sing my longings and my grief to sleep.
It could turn pain to pleasure, and could bring
some sense of harmony to my depression.
But not for long – the doctors put a stop
to that as well; singing was 'bad for one'.
Suffering less so, if it was in silence.
LEONORA:
But now you're well, surrounded by your friends.
PRINCESS:
Well, or – not ill: with lots of friends, true friends,
and that is...very nice. I also used
to have a friend...

59

LEONORA: Still have.
PRINCESS: Until I lose him.
   The moment I first saw him was significant.
   I was just convalescing from…some illness;
   the pain had hardly left me; I was slowly
   coming to life again, daring to look
   into the future, hoping for new friends.
   My sister introduced me to this boy.
   A knot was tied I don't think will unravel.
LEONORA: But why reproach yourself? You found in him
   something that you can never, ever lose.
PRINCESS: One should treat Beauty cautiously, like fire:
   it warms the room, it lights the path – how pretty!
   How could one do without it? Suddenly
   it burns up everything around it. Leave me.
   I talk too much: I should hide, even from you
   how weak and ill I still am.
LEONORA: People's problems
   are always worse for dignified concealment.
PRINCESS: If that's the case, then I shall soon be cured.
   Oh, Leonora, I've decided: yes –
   he goes. But I already feel the numbness,
   the long, drawn-out, ache of days without –
   what gives me happiness. Daylight will not
   remove that beautiful, transfigured, dream-
   impression of him from my waking eyelids:
   the hope of seeing him will no longer fill
   my waking spirit with anticipation:
   my first glance down into the garden will
   seek him in vain among the dew-drenched shadows.
   I wanted to be with him every evening;
   that wish was granted, and it fed the wish
   to know and understand each other better,
   and that companionship tuned both our minds
   to perfect harmony. Now all grows dark,
   the splendour of the sunlight at high noon,
   the myriad varied colours of the world
   are empty, dim and covered by the mist

that now surrounds me. All I ever wanted
was just to see him every single day,
and that day would be like a lifetime to me:
cares were silent, fear itself was dumb,
the stream would carry us on gentle waves,
without our steering. Now the future looms.

LEONORA:
The future will bring him back: you'll find new happiness.

PRINCESS: I want to keep the happiness I've got:
change may be interesting, but hardly useful.
Even when I was young I never felt
the urge to try the lucky dip of Fate
to find, by chance, some unfamiliar object
to set my thirsty, inexperienced heart on.
I saw his genius, and I had to love him.
I had to love him, since with him my life
became life as I'd never known before.
At first I told myself: no, stay away
from him: but then I weakened, and I weakened…
my caution only served to bring us closer.
Well, pleasures will be paid for, and how dearly!
I'm losing something which I really had.
An evil spirit switches joy for pain,
and shews me the dark side of happiness.

LEONORA: If there is nothing I can say to help you,
time and the world are doctors who'll revive you
before you are aware of it.

PRINCESS: Of course,
the world is beautiful, I know, and wide,
and full of life, and wonder, and delight.
Why must it always be one step away?
There is a happiness, but we cannot see it:
or if we can, we don't know what it's worth.
(*She goes out.*)

LEONORA: If she must lose, does that mean I must win?
Is it so needful he should disappear?
Or do I make it needful, so I have
his talent and his heart all to myself

which up to now I've shared with someone else,
and shared unequally. Now, is that fair?
Am I not rich enough? What do I lack?
A husband, children, rank, possessions, beauty –
all these I have already: why should I
want to add him to all that? Do I love him?
Why else is it I cannot give him up?
Confess: you want to see yourself reflected
in Tasso's work: there is a double charm
in being carried away by Art *as well*;
that is the moment when you will be envied.
Not only will you have what others want,
but you will be what others want to be –
the most famous woman in all Italy.
Is only Laura to be celebrated?
Does Petrarch have the copyright to raise
an unknown beauty to divinity?
Would any other poet dare compare
his genius to Tasso's? I think not.
He's famous now: he'll be more so tomorrow.
How glorious, how splendid it would be
to step into the future at his side!
Time, age, and scandal – none of them could touch me.
All that is transient would be preserved
and I would still be beautiful and happy
long after Death had carried me away.
I *must* have him! It is not robbing her;
her liking for him is all of a piece
with all her other passions, like the moon,
which scantily illuminates the path
of travellers by night, but gives no warmth,
creates no pleasure, spreads no joy, no life
around her. She will be as glad to know
he's happy, even if he is not here,
as when she used to see him every day.
And anyway I've not the least intention
of going into banishment with him.
I shall be back, and I shall bring him with me.

Here comes our uncouth friend: now we shall see
if we have charms to soothe his savage breast.
(*Enter ANTONIO.*)
It seems that you have brought us war, not peace.
One might have thought you came here from a battle,
a camp, where violence rules, where fisticuffs
decide things, not from Rome, where Civilisation
kneels willingly to hear and to obey.

ANTONIO: I must accept your criticism, Countess,
    but what you say is, in fact, my excuse.
    Diplomacy and politics can be
    dangerously exhausting in the long run.
    One's evil angel, lurking at one's side,
    demands a sacrifice from time to time:
    this time, unhappily, at a friend's expense.

LEONORA: You've been abroad too long: you have adopted
    foreigner's manners. Now you're back with us
    you treat us all as strangers.

ANTONIO: That's the danger.
    With foreigners one pulls oneself together,
    pays more attention to the little things,
    seeking all the time in their behaviour
    the things that one may use to one's advantage:
    with friends one takes less care, one lets them see
    one's moodiness, relying on their love,
    and all at once one's temper slips the leash,
    and so we injure those we love the most.

LEONORA: That sounds more like the old Antonio.

ANTONIO: I hate myself for what took place today.
    But when one comes back from a galling job,
    'breathless and faint, leaning upon one's sword',
    and finds some idler lying in the shade,
    where one was looking forward to a rest,
    'out of one's grief and one's impatience,
    one says neglectingly, one knows not what'.
    Or is one to be allowed no human feelings?

LEONORA: If one were really human, one'd be glad
    to share the shade with someone else, especially

someone who makes both rest sweet and work easy
with conversation and with music. Come, admit,
the tree is broad, there's room enough for all.
ANTONIO: Eleonora, let's not play with words.
There are many things we gladly share with others.
There's still one thing, though, which we only give
to the deserving, and another thing
which we do *not* share, even *with* the deserving:
namely, a laurel wreath and a woman's love.
LEONORA: You didn't seriously feel the crown
on that boy's head to be some kind of insult?
I can't believe that even you could find
a more discreet reward for his achievement.
Art is intangible, immaterial,
and it can only be rewarded with
symbols and images. And if he himself
hardly ever comes to earth, his head
is just as hardly touched by the award.
It is a dead branch, fitting symbol of
the sterile admiration of his friends,
an easy payment of a difficult debt.
You'd grudge a saint his halo: and a laurel
is more a sign of suffering than happiness.
ANTONIO: Must I learn, from lips as beautiful
as yours, to scorn the vanities of this world?
LEONORA: I'd hardly claim to teach you anything
about the value, or at least, the price
of things. But even wise men must be shewn,
from time to time, like anybody else,
the worth of those things which they own themselves.
Your laurel is the Prince's confidence:
you wear it easily for all its weight,
it suits you well, and God knows you deserve it.
ANTONIO: You do not mention love. Am I to take it
you do not think it all that necessary?
LEONORA: Take it as you will. You hardly feel
the lack of it, and if you did, it would
be easier for you to bear than him.

Now tell me honestly, would any woman
succeed, if she tried to look after you,
as women do? You look after yourself,
just as you look after others. Tasso now,
occupies women in their special sphere.
He always needs a hundred and one things,
the sort of things that women like providing.
Silk shirts, embroidered handkerchiefs – he's most
concerned about his clothes, and everything
must fit just so. But he has no idea
how to get this together, nor of how
to keep it when he has it. He is always
suffering from a chronic shortage, both
of money and responsibility.
Leaving things here and there – he never comes
back from a journey without having lost
at least a third of all of his belongings –
and what he doesn't lose, his servants steal.
We have our hands full with him, all year round.
ANTONIO: And that just makes you love him all the more.
How very fortunate for him to have
his failings counted virtues, and to be
allowed to play the little boy still, at his age.
My dear, you really must forgive me if
I sound a little bitter: but he is
a good deal cleverer than he admits –
or you admit. He has two women's hearts:
he ties the knots of love and then unties them
just as he pleases: is one to believe
such tricks impose on women of your class?
LEONORA: But don't you see, that only goes to prove
that it is only friendship that impels us?
And even if we gave him love for love,
it would be nothing but a fair reward
for someone who lives for his friends, in dreams.
ANTONIO: Continue spoiling him as you are doing,
allow his selfishness to pass for love,
allow him to insult your close acquaintance

without a single word of criticism,
and there will be an end to confidence
in the most intimate circle of your friends.
LEONORA: We're not so partial as you think. We try
to teach him to enjoy himself, so that
he may give others more to enjoy. You must
not think that we are blind to all his faults.
ANTONIO: You do praise much where you should criticise.
I know him – after all, he is transparent,
and far too proud to hide a thing. He is
entirely self-absorbed, and anything
outside him might just as well not exist.
He drops it, pushes it aside, ignores it,
and sits back happily – upon his laurels.
But suddenly an undetected spark
sets off a fuse, he explodes, in pain or joy,
or rage or moodiness, but violently.
At that point he wants everything at once,
to have it, hold it, everything must happen
just as he wants it to: things that require
years of preparation must be there
at once, and things that would need years
of effort to undo must simply be
removed immediately. Then he demands
the impossible of himself so that he can
demand the same of others. And his mind
wants to solve the riddle of the universe.
Well now, I daresay that is possible
for one man in ten million, but not him:
and in the end he falls back none the wiser.
LEONORA: He does no harm to others, just himself.
ANTONIO: That is not true, he does enormous harm
to others. You cannot deny that when
he flies into a passion, he would slander
the Prince, the Princess, anyone at all.
Only a moment maybe, none the less,
moments can be repeated, and he can
no more control his temper than his tongue.

LEONORA: Perhaps if he could leave here for a while,
  both he and we might feel the benefit.
ANTONIO: Perhaps and then again perhaps – not.
  But certainly not now: I do not wish
  to take the blame for it. It could appear
  that I was chasing him away, which I am not.
  As far as I'm concerned, let him stay on,
  and if he wants a reconciliation,
  if he's prepared to follow my advice,
  I daresay we can rub along together.
LEONORA: Now you are thinking you can influence
  a nature you just called a hopeless case.
ANTONIO: One always hopes, it's better than despair.
  Who, after all, can tell just what *is* possible?
  His Highness values him, so we shall keep him.
  And if we fail with him, he will not be
  the only failure we have on our conscience.
LEONORA: That was a sudden change of tune. I don't
  believe you're so dispassionate – or impartial.
ANTONIO: There must be *some* advantage in getting older.
  Even if one can't avoid mistakes,
  one *can* learn to correct them on the spot.
  You wanted me to make my peace with him.
  Now I am asking the same thing of you.
  Do what you can to bring him to his senses,
  and everything can be just as it was.
  I shall go and see him, just as soon
  as you assure me I won't make things worse.
  But if you're going to do it, do it now:
  the Prince is all for going back tonight,
  and I wish to accompany him. Adieu.
  (*ANTONIO goes out.*)
LEONORA: That far, alas, I cannot follow you.
  For once, my friend, our interests do not quite
  go hand-in-hand. I must use what time I have
  in winning Tasso over: now – and quickly!

ACT FOUR

A room.

TASSO: Did you wake from a dream? The vision gone?
    Was it sleep chained you up, and tortured you
    with sights and sounds of fast-receding joy?
    You wake and dream. Where have the hours gone
    when you were crowned with laurel, and the days
    when you could gaze into the sky in freedom?
    And yet you're still alive…and feel. You feel…
    yet can have no assurance you're alive.
    Is it my fault, or his, that I am found
    to be at fault? Is it some crime I have
    committed, which I must atone for? Is
    my whole fault rather not a form of merit?
    Looking at him, I felt impelled towards him,
    both by goodwill and some wild hope of the heart:
    he wore a human face – he must be human.
    But on approaching him with open arms,
    I found no heart, but only bolts and bars.
    And I had thought it out so cleverly,
    how I should greet this man I'd long mistrusted!
    One thing is certain, though – I did see *her*!
    She stood there, spoke to me – I heard her speak!
    Her look, her voice, her words are mine forever:
    not time, nor destiny, nor fortune can
    take that away from me! And if I was
    too hasty, letting the flames be fanned within me
    which now destroy me, I do not regret that;
    even at the price of my salvation,
    I would devote my life to her for ever,
    and follow her along the road to ruin.
    Amen! I showed her I was worthy of
    that trust which gives me life, which gives me life
    at the very hour when the dark gates, giving
    onto a long, long time of grief, are forced wide open.
    Yes, it is finished! and the sun of favour

sets suddenly for me; the Prince has turned
away from me, and now I stand here, lost,
upon a narrow, gloomy path. The hideous
birds of double omen, train of darkness,
swarm out and flap their wings about my head;
where, oh, where can I turn, to flee the horror
surrounding me, oh, how can I avoid
the dark abyss that yawns there at my feet?

LEONORA: (*Entering.*)
What happened then? and how? we're all bewildered.
Did rashness or suspicion drive you to it?
You're normally so gentle, so clear-sighted,
so understanding of what's due to others,
so tolerant, a thing the wise learn quickly,
the stupid never, and so even-tempered.
I hardly know you any more.

TASSO: What if
all that were gone? What if a friend, whom you
had once thought rich, should suddenly turn out
to be a beggar? Yes, you are quite right.
I'm not the man I was, and yet I am.
That isn't quite the riddle that it sounds.
The moon that so enchants us all at night,
is still there in the daytime, but it pales
to insignificance: I have been outshone
by the bright light of day. You do not know
me any more: I do not know myself.

LEONORA: I do not know what you are trying to say,
the way you say it. Are you telling me
that ill-bred man's insulting you has made you
incapable of recognising us
or yourself? Just trust me, Tasso.

TASSO: I am not
the one who's been insulted; I've been punished
for having given the insult. Though the sword
would cut the knot of all those words quite quickly
and easily, I've been made a prisoner.
You cannot think...dear friend, don't be alarmed

69

to find yourself a prison visitor.
The Prince has punished me, just like a schoolboy:
I've no right to complain, and no desire to.
LEONORA: You take it much more seriously than you need.
TASSO: You think I'm such a child that such a punishment
is going to destroy me? I'm not hurt
by what has happened, but by what it means to me.
Let those who hate or envy me betake
themselves to their defence: the field is open.
LEONORA: You entertain too many false suspicions.
Even Antonio does not hate you. What
occurred today between you...
TASSO: ...is forgotten.
I take Antonio as he was and as
he always will be. I have always loathed
that overbearing cleverness, that stiff assumption
of always being in the right: he never
listens, so he will never understand,
but merely smiles at one contemptuously.
Well, I am not so old – yet – nor so clever
that I'll accept being smiled at, and smile back.
Sooner or later there was bound to be
a quarrel: any later and it would
have been much worse. I recognise one master,
the one who pays my wages, whom I follow
gladly; I neither need nor want another.
I want freedom to think and to create.
There are enough restrictions in this world.
LEONORA: Antonio speaks well of you, and often.
TASSO: You mean he speaks of me with kind forbearance –
refined and – oh! – so clever. That's what stings.
Praise in his mouth becomes as bad as blame.
LEONORA: You should have heard him praise your genius:
he recognises it for what it's worth.
TASSO: And what is that supposed to mean? Believe me,
self-centred souls like his cannot escape
the lash of envy. Men like that forgive you
for having fortune, rank or reputation,

because they think 'I could do that myself,
if I just made the effort.' What they can't
and won't forgive in you is anything
that comes from Nature, things that can't be got
by industry or application, nor
by money, trickery, will-power or brute force.
He recognise my talent? A man who thinks
he can cajole the Muses with a bludgeon?
A critic fancying himself an artist,
because he's learnt to string the thoughts together
he steals from other artists? He would sooner
see me in favour with the Prince – and that
is something he would rather see reserved
for himself – than ever he'd admit the Muses
had smiled on some poor, wretched, common orphan.

LEONORA: You're wrong about him: he is not like that.

TASSO: To be wrong about him is a real pleasure.
I would be sorry if I thought of him
in any other than the way I do:
I think it's stupid being fair in everything.
It just destroys our individuality.
Are people fair to us? No, they are not.
Within the narrow compass of our natures
we need both love and hate, both night and day,
waking and sleeping. From now on I must
keep him before me, to personify
my deepest hatred: nothing can remove
the pleasure of detesting him more and more.

LEONORA: If you persist in thinking in this way,
I hardly see how you can stay at court.
You know how valuable they think he is.

TASSO: As valuable as I've become superfluous.

LEONORA: That you are not, nor ever like to be.

TASSO:
Oh, no? When did the Prince once take me seriously?

LEONORA: Don't be ungrateful. Setting you free of all
official duties is a compliment.

TASSO: He sets me free because he finds me useless.

71

LEONORA: It is by being free you are most use.
    You hug resentment to you like a child.
    I've often thought – I cannot help myself –
    this splendid soil where Fate's transplanted you,
    is stony ground for you; you do not flourish.
    Tasso, you want to know my own opinion?
    Of course you don't, but here it is; I think –
    I think that you should leave here for a while.
TASSO: Don't spare the patient, doctor. Twist the knife.
    Give him the medecine: never mind if it
    is bitter – ask yourself 'Will he recover?'
    I see quite clearly now that all is over.
    I forgive him – which is more than he does for me.
    Antonio wishes to supplant me here.
    He fills a need at court, which I do not.
    He is a clever man, which I am not.
    My friends, who could stand up for me, desert me.
    You think I ought to leave: I think so too:
    goodbye: since you've a mind to part from me,
    I hope I find the strength to part from you.
LEONORA: Distance will lend enchantment to the view,
    and clarify what seems bewildering.
    Perhaps you'll realise that, after all,
    you were surrounded here by love, and learn
    to know the value of good friends, and see
    the outside world's no substitute for friendship.
TASSO: We'll see. I grew up in the real world.
    I know how it can leave you destitute
    and alone, continuing blithely on its way
    like the sun, or moon, or any other gods.
LEONORA: Listen to me, and you will never have
    to go through that experience again.
    Join us in Florence. I am going there
    myself, in a day or two, to join my husband,
    and there is nothing I can think of that
    we'd rather do than welcome you to our circle.
    Need I say more? You know the kind of prince
    my husband is, the kind of men and women

that Florence cultivates. Nothing to say?
Will you? Well, think it over, then decide.
TASSO: Everything you say is so attractive,
    so much in keeping with my secret dreams.
    It's all so new: please – give me time to think,
    I will decide soon.
LEONORA: I shall leave you then,
    with hope – for you, for us, and for this house.
TASSO: Just one thing more: how does the Princess feel?
    Was she annoyed with me? What did she say?
    Does she in any way blame me? Please be frank.
LEONORA:
    She knows you well enough by now: she can forgive you.
TASSO: Have I lost favour? Do not lie to me.
LEONORA: A woman's favour's not so lightly lost.
TASSO: Will she be glad to see me go away?
LEONORA: Of course she will, if it's to your advantage.
TASSO: Won't I be losing favour with the Prince?
LEONORA: I think you can rely on his largesse.
TASSO: But can we leave the Princess on her own?
    You will be leaving soon: and though I don't
    mean much to her, I know I do mean something.
LEONORA: An absent friend is still a friend – the more so
    if we are sure he's happy, and you will be.
    This will succeed, and honour will be satisfied.
    The Prince has told Antonio to apologise.
    So – please – receive him calmly when he comes.
TASSO: I'm not in any way ashamed to meet him.
LEONORA: If I could make you see, before you leave,
    no one in Italy hates you, persecutes you,
    or forges secret plots do you harm.
    You are so wrong. You make such joy for others,
    yet at the same time your imagination
    spins such strange webs to trap and hurt yourself.
    I shall do everything I can to break them,
    to give you some chance to enjoy your life.
    Goodbye. I hope you make the right decision.
    (*She goes.*)

TASSO: So I'm to recognise nobody hates me,
    nobody persecutes me, those conspiracies
    are all imagination, in my head.
    I'm to admit that I was in the wrong,
    that I'd wronged others who did not deserve it!
    This at a time when both my right and their
    deceitfulness are clear as day!
    I'm to be grateful for the Prince's favour,
    just when his eyes are blinded and his hands
    are fettered by my enemies. And I? –
    am to hold my tongue, so they may comfortably
    continue their deception, quite unnoticed.
    I'm to be dumb. Who gave me that advice?
    Leonora Sanvitale, my good friend.
    Well, now I know her, why did I ever trust her?
    Basically it was vanity made me do so,
    thinking she was deceiving all the others,
    but me. Now Fortune's turned her back on me,
    and Leonora follows her example.
    She comes now as the tool of those who hate me,
    a smooth-tongued serpent, hissing her enchantment.
    She seemed so lovely, spoke so lovingly,
    but flattery could not long conceal her falsehood.
    The contrary to everything she said
    was all too clearly written on her face.
    I'm quick to spot attempts to find a way
    into my heart, that don't come *from* the heart.
    So! I'm to leave for Florence, then! And soon!
    Why Florence? I can see that quite distinctly.
    The new house of the Medici is in power,
    and while they are not in open enmity,
    the silent chill of envy still divides them.
    If, as I may assume, the Dukes of Tuscany
    would welcome me with every sign of favour,
    Antonio would soon be casting doubt
    upon my loyalty and slurs on my
    devotion – it would be so easy for him!
    Oh, I shall leave, but not in the way you want:

I shall go far, much further than you think.
What keeps me here? Why should I stay? I wormed
the truth from Leonora; I caught the drift.
I know exactly what the Princess thinks:
'Will she be glad to see me go away?'
'Of course she will, if it's to your advantage.'
I wish there were some feeling in her heart
she would destroy both me and my advantage.
I would far sooner die than be dismissed
with a cold wave of the hand. But I shall go,
taking good care that I am not deceived
by so-called friends. Nobody can deceive you,
the moment that you cease to deceive yourself.

ANTONIO: (*Entering.*) Here I am, Tasso, ready to talk to you,
    if you're prepared, or capable of listening.

TASSO: You know quite well I'm not in a position
    to choose: my duty is to wait and listen.

ANTONIO: I'm glad to find you so composed: I can
    speak openly. First, in the Prince's name,
    I am commanded to release you from
    the mild restrictions recently imposed
    upon your liberty.

TASSO: I was imprisoned
    by one caprice, and now I am released
    by another. Good! I seek no further justice.

ANTONIO: It seems that I offended you, and more,
    by what I said, more than I realised. I
    was prey to various conflicting feelings.
    But let me say no unconsidered word
    of insult crossed my lips. You have no need
    to ask for an apology, as a gentleman.
    But as a man, you surely won't refuse one.

TASSO: I shan't ask which hurts most, insult or scorn.
    One tears the skin, the other cuts to the bone.
    The barb of insult turns back on the sender:
    a sword, well-handled, can redress opinion,
    but an offended heart finds no redress.

ANTONIO: I see I must ask you not to reject my offer.
    Do not refuse. It is the Prince's wish.

TASSO: In which case, I, of course, shall do my duty:
and pardon everything that can be pardoned.
There is a story of a magic spear
with the power to heal the wounds that it inflicts.
The human tongue has much the same effect;
nor shall I be so rude as to reject it.

ANTONIO: Thank you. I wish you'd make a trial of me
and my desire to help you. Is there nothing
that I can do for you?

TASSO: You brought me back
my freedom: now find me opportunity
to put it to some use.

ANTONIO: How do you mean?

TASSO: As you must be aware, my work is now
finished, if not by any means completed.
I gave it to the Prince today, in hope
that I might at the same time ask a favour.
So many of my friends are now in Rome:
they've commented on a lot of passages:
I've found their letters useful, but there are
still many places where I wait to be
convinced before I make the alterations
they have suggested. But this cannot all
be done by correspondence: such solutions
are easier reached when one is on the spot.
I found no chance to ask the Prince this morning:
and now I daren't, unless it comes from you.

ANTONIO: I think you'd be unwise to leave just now.
The fact that you have reached some sort of ending
commends you to the Prince – and to his sister.
A day of favour's like a day of harvest;
the sheaves must be brought in while they are ripe.
Absence will gain you nothing, and may lose you
what you've already gained. The present is
a powerful goddess. Learn to recognise
your influence, and your advantage. Stay.

TASSO: But what have I to fear? Alfonso is
noble and generous, or at least to me:

and as for what I hope, I shall not grovel,
nor take a thing he might regret he'd given.
ANTONIO: Then do not ask him for your *congé* now:
he will resent it, and I fear, refuse it.
TASSO: He'll give it gladly, if approached correctly,
and you're the man can do it, if you want to.
ANTONIO: On what grounds, pray?
TASSO: Just let my work speak
                                                                    for me.

Even if I have not achieved the goal
I set myself, a man's reach should exceed
his grasp, or what's a heaven for? Alfonso
appreciates ambition, toil and sweat.
The happy traffic of so many days,
the silent spaces of so many nights,
all dedicated to completion of
a work of such devotion, where I sought
to approach the masters of a former time,
and rouse our sleepy age to heroism.
But if it is to wake the best in men,
it must be worthy of the best in me.
Up to now, everything in the work I owe
to him: I'd like to thank him for the ending.
ANTONIO: Yes, but the Prince is *here*, as are others
who can advise you quite as well as Rome:
Ferrara is the place to finish it,
then take it to Rome, to make its full effect.
TASSO: The Prince was first to give an impulse to
my work, and he will be its final judge.
The opinions of those clever men here at court,
such as yourself, I find most valuable;
and if my friends should be unable to
persuade me finally to go to Rome,
then you shall be my judges; but I must
consult them all the same. Gonzaga has
convened a whole Academy for me.
I cannot miss it. I can hardly wait.
Flaminio de' Nobili, Angelio

    da Barga, Antoniano and Speroni!
    You'll know them all – what names! They fill my mind
    with confidence, if also apprehension;
    their judgment I would happily submit to.

ANTONIO: You think of self, self, self. He will not grant it,
    or if so, with reluctance. Do you want me
    to plead for you against my better judgment?

TASSO: You ask me to make trial of your friendship:
    and then refuse the very first thing I ask.

ANTONIO: You strike one at this moment as a man
    who thinks that anything he wants is good,
    and anything he thinks desirable
    has to be done immediately, if not sooner.
    Haste makes waste. Only a lunatic
    would think of using violence to do
    the work of strength and truth. Duty demands
    I moderate, as far as I am able,
    the indecent haste that does you so much harm.

TASSO: I have long thought the tyranny of friendship,
    the most obnoxious tyranny of all.
    But you think differently, so you think
    you're right. But even if I grant you seek
    my good, you need not guide my every step.

ANTONIO: I give you my opinion, in cold blood:
    and even that you think is harmful to you?

TASSO: Set your mind at rest upon that score.
    You say I'm free, the Prince's door stands open.
    The choice is yours. The Prince is leaving soon.
    There is no time to lose. If you do not
    see him, I shall, whatever the result.

ANTONIO: Just let me ask you for a little time!
    Wait till the Prince returns. Just not today!

TASSO: No, it must be at once if possible!
    This marble pavement burns my feet: my mind
    will find no rest until the dust of travel
    swirls round me. I implore you! You can see
    how clumsy I would be in speaking to
    my master at this moment – how can I hide it? –

no power on earth could, at this moment, have
control of me, that have none of myself.
Chains are the only things that could restrain me.
Alfonso is no tyrant – he released me!
How gladly I obeyed him in the past!
Today, though, I can not – just for today,
leave me my freedom, to find myself again.
I shall soon regain my sense of duty.

ANTONIO: What should I do? You place me in some doubt.
Should I assume your error is contagious?

TASSO: If I'm to think you have my interest
at heart, do what I ask, as best you can.
The Prince will let me go. I shall not lose
his aid and favour, which I'll owe to you.
I shall be grateful. But, if you harbour still
a grudge, and wish me banished from the court,
if you want to destroy me, drive me out
into the world, let us remain at odds,
if you rate your opinion over my friendship.

ANTONIO: Since I seem bound to hurt you either way,
I'd better follow your suggestion.
You wish to leave. But let me tell you now:
the minute you turn your back upon this house,
you'll wish you were back inside it once again.
And while your heart will ache for your return,
your stubbornness will drive you on to Rome,
where pain, confusion and depression wait
to welcome you, and you will miss your aim
as surely there as here. I'm telling you,
that is just what will happen, and I ask you,
when my worst fears are realised, that you trust me.
I shall now speak to the Prince, as you command.
(*Exit.*)

TASSO: Yes, go, then! Go, secure in the conviction
that you have talked me round to what you want.
I learn hypocrisy fast – but I've been taught
by masters, and they've found a willing pupil.
Life forces us to appear, indeed to *be*
like those we ought most to despise. I see

the whole plot now. Antonio wants to drive
me out of here, while seeming not to do so.
He acts my guardian angel so that they
will think I am incompetent and sick.
He appoints himself my guardian, so he can
humiliate me like a naughty child,
since he cannot make me a willing slave.
And so the Prince and Princess are deceived.
He thinks that they should keep me: after all,
Nature has given me some noble gifts,
but sadly laden me with weaknesses
to counterweigh her generosity:
exaggerated sensitivity,
unbounded pride, a gloomy cast of mind.
I can do nothing for it. Destiny
has cast this man in this particular mould,
and they must take him just the way he is,
put up with him, endure him, and perhaps
one day, an unexpected benefit,
enjoy some sudden pleasure he can bring them:
but for the rest, the man must be allowed
to live and work and die as he was born.
Do I see here Alfonso's steadfast mind,
shielding his friends and challenging his foes?
The man who now confronts me – do I know him?
I see now the extent of my disaster.
My fate must be that all those who stay firm
and loyal to their friends, will change to me,
easily, at a breath, a moment's notice.
Antonio's return, in one short hour,
destroyed the fabric of my happiness,
and undermined the whole foundation of it!
That I should have to find this out, today!
Yes, just as everyone once thronged to me,
now I am utterly rejected by them.
All those who sought to draw me to their side
and hold me, now avoid me, cast me off.
And why? Does that man alone outweigh

my merit and that love I once enjoyed?
Yes, all flies from me now. You too, you too,
Princess – did you, in this dark hour, send me
one single signal of your sympathy?
Did I deserve that from you? My poor heart
found it so natural to worship her:
to hear her voice, or just to hear her name
spoken by strangers, made my heart stand still.
And words could not express the joy I felt
simply knowing I loved her. Now she too...
At sight of her, daylight grew dim for me;
her eye, her lip, would irresistibly
draw me to her, my knees would scarce support me,
I needed all my strength of mind to stay
standing, and not fall prostrate at her feet,
so hard was it to resist this ecstasy.
Then let my heart be strong now, my mind clear!
She too! Dare I say it? And believe it?
Oh, I believe it – would I could pass it over!
She too! She too! However you excuse her,
do not conceal it from yourself. She too! She too!
I ought to doubt those words, as long as I've
a breath of hope or faith left in my body.
Those words, though, like some grim decree of Fate,
are etched into the margin of my book
of torment, densely printed as it is.
Now suddenly my enemies are strong,
and all my strength is taken from me for ever.
How can I fight, if she has joined the ranks
of the opposing armies? How can I
go on, if she no longer reaches out
her hand to help me? If her eyes do not
meet mine, that beg for help? I had the courage
to picture it, to put it into words:
now it has happened, sooner than I feared.
Now then, before despair takes hold of you
and claws your senses, realise your fate,
and say those words once more: She too! She too!

ACT FIVE

ANTONIO: I spoke to Tasso, for the second time,
    at your suggestion. I've just come from him.
    He will not change his mind, and still insists
    you give him leave to go away to Rome.
DUKE: I've seldom been so vexed with anyone:
    I must admit, and better admit to you
    than anybody else, or I'll be angrier.
    He wants to leave? Good. I shall not detain him.
    He wants to go away? To Rome? So be it.
    Just let's ensure that Scipio Gonzaga,
    that devious Medici does not contrive
    to steal him from me. That is what has made
    Italy great, the rivalry of neighbours,
    to get the best men and make the best use of them.
    A Prince who fails to gather talent round him,
    is like a general without an army;
    the man whose mind will not respond to art, is
    a barbarian, I don't care who he is.
    As far as Tasso is concerned, I found him,
    I'm proud to have him in my household, and
    considering what I've done for him already,
    I've no intention now of losing him.
ANTONIO: I feel somewhat embarrassed, as I was
    partly to blame for what took place today.
    But, as for my effecting a *rapprochement*,
    I hope you will believe I did my best.
DUKE: No, rest assured, Antonio, I never
    held any of this against you. I well know
    the nature of the boy, and what I did,
    how much I shielded him, how much ignored
    his own responsibility in the matter.
    We can master many things within ourselves,
    but neither time nor cruel necessity
    will ever change the way we really are.
ANTONIO: When others do so much for someone, then
    it's only just he ask himself 'What can
    I do for them?' Does that occur to him?

DUKE: Peace is not made to last for long. Just when
    we think we're safe, God sends a foe to try
    our courage, or a friend to try our patience.
ANTONIO: Does he even fulfil the basic duty,
    the thing that first distinguished men from beasts,
    choosing his food? He grabs at everything
    he wants, just like a child: sweet things, spices,
    strong liquor, one after the other, down the hatch.
    Then he complains of melancholy, blames
    his violent destiny! Pure indigestion:
    allied to galloping hypochondria.
    It would be funny if it weren't pathetic.
    I've often heard him talking to the doctor:
    'I have this pain. Can you suggest a cure?'
    'Yes, avoid such and such.'
                           'I couldn't do that.'
    'Then take this twice a day.'
                            'It tastes disgusting.
    How could I possibly?'
                      'Drink water then.'
    'Water? You must be mad, I shun the stuff
    like a man with rabies.'
                      'In which case, I can
    do nothing for you.'
                    'But whyever not?'
    'Your sickness will increase, and though it won't
    carry you off exactly, still the pain
    can only get worse.'
                  'Charming, I must say.
    What sort of doctor do you call yourself?
    You see how ill I am, so you should know
    something you could prescribe which tastes delicious,
    or else the cure's more painful than the illness.'
    You smile, but it's quite true. You must have heard him.
DUKE: Often, and excused it far too often.
ANTONIO: Clearly an irregular way of life
    not only creates nightmares, but breeds daydreams.
    Where else do all these dark suspicions come from?
    He sees himself perpetually surrounded

by enemies, all envying his talent,
as everybody must, of course, and envy
means hatred, plots and bitter persecution.
How often has he bothered you with tales
of locks being forced, his mail being steamed open,
plots to assassinate him even? And when you
look into it, you find what? Not a trace.
How can you shelter somebody like that,
or hope to get much pleasure from his presence?
Far better surely if he went away.
DUKE: You might be right, Antonio, if I were
seeking my own immediate advantage
in him. It certainly is an advantage
not to expect a tangible return
on my investment in him, all at once
or unconditionally. Everything
is useful to us in a different way.
The man who needs much will have many servants,
and use them all to see he is well served.
The Medicis have taught us that; so have
the Popes. What patience, what forbearance
those princes showed in dealing with great talents
who seemed not to need their help, but did in practice!
ANTONIO: Which of us can fail to be aware
of that, my Lord? We know life is a struggle
and if it teaches us one thing, it is
the value of the goods of life, and Tasso
has had both far too much and far too young
for him to appreciate them properly.
He really needs to earn what he's now offered
so open-handedly: he would exert
himself, which would eventually
make him much happier. But when a prince
makes a poor nobleman a courtier,
relieving him from poverty, that is
the crown and summit of the fellow's wishes.
If, further, he receives his confidence
and favour, and promotion over others,

whether in war, business, or merely talk,
then I'd have thought the modest man would show
his happiness in silent gratitude.
But Tasso's had all this and more: he has
his country's recognition and its hopes.
His moods and sulks are all attributable
to the soft feather-bedding of success.
He's coming. Now, Sire, give him leave and time
to go to Rome, or Naples, or wherever,
to look for what he thinks he misses here,
and what he'll only find when he gives up
the search and comes back here.

DUKE: Does he want first to go back to Ferrara?

ANTONIO: He wants to stay on here in Belriguardo.
   A friend will send on what he needs.

DUKE: Agreed then.
   My sister and Leonora will be leaving
   immediately, but I can overtake them.
   You follow, once you've taken care of Tasso.
   See that the steward provides him with whatever
   he needs to stay here at the castle, till
   his friends have sent his luggage on, and till
   I can arrange the letters of introduction
   he'll need for Rome. But here he is. Farewell.
   (*ANTONIO leaves. Enter TASSO.*)

TASSO: (*With reserve.*) I never fully appreciated all
   the kindness you have shown me till today.
   My thoughless, criminal actions, in your presence,
   you have forgiven, reconciled me to
   my opponent. If I ask you now for leave
   to spend some time away from here, I hope
   that you will not withdraw your patronage.
   I'm confident that Time will heal all ills.

DUKE: I hope it may: I wish you luck: I hope
   you will come back to us both cured and happy.
   I'll give you letters to my friends in Rome,
   and hope you'll make good use of them – and trust them.
   Even abroad, I still see you as mine.

TASSO: You overwhelm me, Sire, I find no words
    to thank you at the moment. But instead
    of thanks, may I ask one more favour?
    My work is nearest and dearest to my heart.
    I've spent much time and effort on it, but
    there's still a lot to do, and I should like
    to go to school again, to learn in Rome,
    where the inspiration of great minds is felt
    and felt effectively; then what I write
    will be the worthier of the praise you give it.
    Will you return the manuscript I gave you,
    which I now blush to know is in your hands?
DUKE: You really are a fellow of rare gifts –
    in every sense: you surely cannot wish me
    to give you back what I received today?
    Let me be middleman between your work
    and you: you must beware of damaging
    its life and delicacy by too much effort.
    Don't listen to advice from every hand.
    The artist's business is to reconcile
    the contradictory opinions of
    many different men, and not be shy
    of giving offence to many, so he can
    the better please the audience he wants.
    Mind you, I won't say here and there a bit
    of polishing might not come amiss. I'll have
    a copy made of this, and sent to you.
    The original, in your hand, stays in mine.
    So that I can enjoy it properly with
    my sisters. If you bring it back from Rome
    the more improved, our pleasure will be the more:
    if we have criticisms, they will be
    the products both of frankness and of friendship.
TASSO: I must ask you again, albeit with
    a certain shame, to let me have it back.
    My whole life now is centred on that work.
    I have to make it what it has to be.
DUKE: Your energy is laudable, but, my dear
    good Tasso, if it's possible, you should

take a short holiday; enjoy yourself;
go to a spa – it purifies the blood.
Things will fall into place, which now must seem
irreconcilable with one another.

TASSO: Perhaps, Your Highness, but I'm only well
when I can get on with my work. You know
I hate being idle; ease makes me uneasy.
Unfortunately Nature did not intend me
to drift on aimlessly towards eternity.

DUKE: Every single thing you think or do,
leads you back to yourself. You must take care.
There are a good many pits surrounding us,
dug by Fate: the deepest of all is here
inside us, and we find a strange attraction
in throwing ourselves in. I beg you, try
to separate, detach yourself from…Tasso.
The artist's loss will be the real man's gain.

TASSO: Life is no longer life without my work.
There is no way you can forbid the silkworm
to spin, although he spins himself to death:
he weaves the splendid web from his own entrails,
and only stops when he has spun his shroud.
How enviable! If only God would give us
a fate like that, so we could spread our wings
with sudden joy in some new sun-drenched valley!

DUKE: Listen to me now: you give countless people
a double joy in life – now will you learn
to recognise the value of that life,
which you possess ten times more vividly
than others? Well, goodbye. And *bon voyage.*
The sooner back, the better pleased we'll be.
(*Exit DUKE.*)

TASSO: There. I was right. Hold firm. But it was hard.
The first time you have had to play the hypocrite
to that extent: it proves that you can do it.
That wasn't his true nature, not a word
he spoke was his: I heard Antonio's voice
echo in every syllable. From now on

I shall be hearing it on every hand.
I must be firm. An instant could decide.
Learning hypocrisy so late in life
has one advantage: one can still *look* honest.
All will be well – begin to practice on them.
I spoke too soon. The Princess comes. Oh God!
Anger and suspicion fuse to pain.

PRINCESS: (*Entering.*) I hear you mean to leave us: not, I hope
for very long. You're going to Rome?

TASSO: At first.
I need some time off to complete my work.
There are so many men in Rome who can
be called the masters of their art. Rome is
the capital of the world, and every stone
speaks to us, countless silent teachers who
welcome us, solemn and majestic. If
I cannot finish my work there, then where?
But I'm afraid no work of mine will ever
meet with good fortune: change, but not completion.
Art should sustain us all, and healthy minds
are strengthened and encouraged by it, but
I feel it all too clearly that it will
be my undoing – it will drive me out.
And on to Naples.

PRINCESS: But you can't go there!
Are you not still an exile, like your father?

TASSO: You're right to warn me, but I've thought of that.
I shall go in disguise, dressed as a pilgrim
or as a peasant, hurry through the city
where one man can be swallowed in the crowd,
Get to the river, find a boat that brings
the peasants back from market to Sorrento:
that's where my sister lives, who was, with me
the certain sorrow and uncertain joy
of our poor parents. I shall disembark
in silence, ask directions: some old crone
will point me out the street. I'll climb on up.
The children will be playing round about,

and staring at the wild-haired, sad-eyed stranger.
The door is standing open, I go in...
PRINCESS: Open your eyes, if such a thing is possible,
and see the risks those fantasies could cause.
I am too soft with you, or I should say:
is it quite fair of you to talk like that
to think like that, entirely of yourself,
without considering your friends at all?
Have you no inkling how my brother feels?
Or how I feel myself? Is that all changed?
Go if you must, but don't leave us like this.
(*TASSO turns away.*)
When friends go on a journey, however brief,
it's comforting if we can give them something,
even if just a new coat, or a weapon.
But there is nothing I can give you, Tasso,
you throw away everything that you possess.
You choose a pilgrim's cloak and staff, and go
in self-elected poverty, all you take
is the pleasure only we could share with you.
TASSO: You do not utterly reject me then?
How good that is to hear, how wonderful.
Let me stay here in Belriguardo, or
send me to Consandoli – where you will.
The Prince has many houses, all with gardens,
which need attention twelve months in the year;
you hardly set foot in them for a day,
an hour even. Choose the furthest off,
the one you never see for years on end,
neglected, half in ruins, send me there.
Let me slave for you there – care for the trees,
protect the lemon trees with boards in autumn,
and bind them up with straw. Plant the beds
with flowers, weed the walks, sweep every corner.
And let me keep the palace; see the windows
are opened at the proper times, so that
the damp does not get at the paintings: dust
the plasterwork in every nook and cranny.

The attic will be scrubbed and gleam with polish,
no stone or tile will be in disrepair,
no blade of grass will grow in any crack.

PRINCESS: I find no words to help you or advise you,
I find no comfort here for you – or us.
I look around to see if there's a God
can help us, or some opiate, some drug
to bring some peace to your mind, and my own.
But all the words and all the medicines
mean nothing now. I have to say goodbye:
but my heart cannot do it.

TASSO: Oh, my God,
say something, anything. What shall I do?
So that the prince, your brother, will forgive me,
so that you yourself may be inclined
to forgive me, so that I can once again
account myself your friend, and live among you?

PRINCESS: It is so little that we want from you,
and yet it seems it is too much to ask.
We do not ask you to be what you're not:
we ask you to accept just what you are.
You make us happy when we see you happy:
and you depress us when you run away
from happiness. If we become impatient
it is because we only want to help you,
and see, alas, that you will not be helped.
You will not take the friendly hand that's offered;
however far we stretch, it does not reach you.

TASSO: Forgive my human weakness, that I failed
to recognise the angel whom I met
so long ago. I know that I shall never
feel joy like this again. Only this feeling
can ever make me happy on this earth;
and only it can ever make me wretched
if I resist it, try to blot it out.
I thought I could control it, fight against it,
I struggled with myself, almost destroying
that self, that utterly belongs to you...

PRINCESS: If I'm to listen to you any longer, then
    you must not say such things. You frighten me.
TASSO: Is it the glass's fault the wine runs over?
    With every word you raise my happiness.
    With every word you say your eyes shine brighter.
    I feel such change inside me, feel a burden
    is lifted from my shoulders. I am free
    as God himself, and thank you for it all.
    A power I can't describe flows from your lips
    and over-masters me, and from now on
    nothing remains of me that is not yours.
    My tongue is heavy and my senses fail,
    thin fire steals through me, darkness shrouds my eyes.
    You draw me irresistibly towards you,
    my heart is now no longer in my power.
    You have me now for ever. Take my life.
    (*He falls into her arms and holds her close.*)
PRINCESS: (*Pushing him away and hurrying out.*)
    Get away from me!
LEONORA: (*Who has been visible in the background for a
    while, now hurries forward.*)
                    What's happening? Tasso!
    (*She goes out after the PRINCESS.*)
TASSO: (*About to follow them.*)
    Oh, God!
DUKE: (*Who has been seen approaching with ANTONIO.*)
          The boy is mad. See him looked after.
    (*The PRINCE goes out.*)
ANTONIO: If any of the enemies you always
    imagine to be surrounding you were here
    right at this moment, he would be delighted.
    Poor man! I need a moment to recover.
    When we meet something wholly unexpected,
    or witness something monstrous happening,
    we stand there for a moment paralysed,
    because we have no basis for comparison.
TASSO: (*After a long pause.*)
    I see you like your job, so do your duty.
    You do indeed deserve the Prince's trust:

now that the rod is broken over me,
fulfil your office, then, and martyr me;
a lingering death; first let me feel the edge
and see the instrument that must despatch me.
You are a fitting tool of tyranny,
as goaler, torturer, or what you will,
how well, how perfectly the roles become you.
(*Speaking into the wings.*)
Well, tyrant! You may go – you could not hide
your true intent indefinitely – enjoy
your triumph, now the slave is safely chained,
and spared for cunningly imagined tortures.
Go! Tyranny disgusts me, when it acts
both against justice and religion.
(*After a pause.*)
So in the end I'm thrown out like a beggar!
That's why they crowned me – so I could be led
with garlands to the sacrificial altar.
At the last moment, though, he cheated me;
he stole my work, the only thing I owned.
My only property is now in *your* hands,
which would have been my passport to the world,
the only thing between me and starvation.
I see why I was urged to take a rest.
Conspiracy, and you were at its head!
So that my work would never be completed,
so that my name would never become famous,
so that my critics could batten on my weaknesses
with envious tongues, and let me be forgotten.
Such care for me, such selfless altruism!
And the Princess, I see her now – too late –
a siren set to sing me to my ruin.
Oh, why do we deceive ourselves so willingly?
Flattering those we should despise, in hope
they'll flatter us. Men do not know each other:
only galley-slaves know each other, chained together
on a narrow bench, where no one makes demands,
and nobody has anything to lose,

where everyone admits he is a rogue,
and knows his next door neighbour is one too.
But we pretend politely to ignore
our neighbours, in the hope they'll do the same.
How long the saintly icon she constructed
concealed the truth about the courtesan
and all her little tricks! Now the mask falls,
and I can see Armida, with her charms
all stripped away, just as I described her
with what I must think was presentiment.
Oh, and the artful little go-between,
Leonora!
Hearing the rustle of her footsteps now,
I find her quite despicable, now I know
the circle that she crept around so slyly.
But now I know you all. And let that be
satisfaction enough for me: and if
my misery robs me of everything,
I value it for shewing me the truth.

ANTONIO: I listen to you with astonishment.
I know your hasty spirit swings from one
extreme to another. Pull yourself together.
Control your anger. You allow yourself
libels for which you may forgive your pain,
but for which you never will forgive yourself.

TASSO: Don't flatter me, and spare me your advice.
Let me preserve the luxury of gloom:
I do not wish to be brought to my senses
only to lose them, as a criminal
is kept in hospital until he's well
enough for them to hang him. I must go:
and if you are my friend, as you insist,
then prove it now, and let me go in peace.

ANTONIO: I certainly shall not abandon you
in this condition: and if you collapse,
you will not find me doing so in sympathy.

TASSO: Then must I yield myself your prisoner?
All right, I yield, and there's the business ended.
I shall make no resistance: I'm content.

Now you can leave me to persuade myself
how beautiful it all was, what I've lost.
Is that them leaving now? God! I can see
the dust already, from their carriage-wheels –
the outriders go on ahead. They've gone.
I came here with them, now they leave without me.
In anger too. If I could kiss his hand
just one more time, just to say goodbye!
Just to say once again, 'Forgive me!'; just
to hear him saying, 'Go! You are forgiven!'
But I don't hear it, and I never will.
I want to leave! But let me say goodbye –
only goodbye. Just let me, for a moment,
recognise their presence in the present!
Perhaps I shall be well again – who knows?
No! No! I am cast off, discarded, exiled:
I have exiled myself: I'll never hear
her voice again, nor see her face, nor meet...

ANTONIO: Do not surrender quite so easily.
Remember you have someone at your side
who is not wholly without sympathy.
Your pain is not so great as you believe.

TASSO: But is it what it seems? Am I as weak
as I have shewn myself? Have I lost everything?
Has pain, like an earthquake, shrunk my world
to a handful of dust? Is all my talent gone?
Nothing inside me to distract me and
support me? No more strength? There's nothing left –
nothing at all.
No, everything's still there, it's I who am nothing.
She has been stolen from me, I from myself!

ANTONIO: If everything's still there, adjust yourself
to that, and find a balance with the world.
Try to see yourself for what you are!

TASSO: A timely reminder: has History no more
examples to instruct us? Is there no
hero of legend to stand there before me
whose sufferings were greater than my own?
To whom I may compare myself and be

94

a man? No, that's all past. One thing remains:
Nature has given us the gift of tears,
the cry of pain, when suffering becomes
unbearable. She gives that to us all,
but in addition, maybe to make up
for the greater degree of pain some people suffer,
she gives them power to express that pain,
in song or speech, and by expressing, dull it.
And if most men are speechless in their sorrow,
some God at least gave me the power to speak.
(*ANTONIO goes to him and takes his hand.*)
Oh, my good friend, you stand there, strong and silent,
and I am nothing but a storm-tossed wave.
But do not overestimate your power.
All-powerful Nature may have fixed the rock,
but her same power gave movement to the wave.
She sends the storm, the wave retreats and trembles
and swells and bows its head in foam, and breaks.
In the wave that was myself, the sun
would gaze on its reflection, and the stars
would rest upon my shoulder, rocked to sleep.
That peace is gone, the glory is departed.
Danger has rendered me incapable
of recognising my own image, but
I can confess the fact now, without shame.
The helm is shattered, and the vessel splits.
The deck cracks open underneath my feet.
I clutch you, my salvation, with both hands,
just as a drowning sailor grabs at last
the rock that should have brought about his ruin.

The End.

CLAVIGO
A Tragedy in Five Acts

Introduction

In a lifetime of taking the theatre more, or quite often, rather less than seriously, Goethe produced a hugely varied, and spasmodically triumphant body of work for it. For a man referred to, some time later as 'the last universal man', Goethe's early dramatic work covers a surprising number of false starts, abandoned fragments, and general dramatic doodling, hovering between the pretentious and the crass, until, in 1773, still in his early twenties, he hit his stride, and wrote in quick succession a number of works that made him an author to be noticed.

First of these was *Goetz von Berlichingen*, an ambitious historical canvas of late mediaeval barons, knights and thugs. The only one of his plays to achieve great and general applause on its first appearance, it was painstakingly written and rewritten in several versions, in marked contrast to his later practice. Indeed, his next production and even greater success, was not a play but a novel, which took him, he tells us, a bare four weeks to write. *Werther* appeared the following year, his twenty-fourth, and as near to overnight as makes no difference made him the most famous writer in Europe: any one of a certain age who could read hurried to dress in blue cutaways and yellow waistcoats, cry a good deal, and occasionally shoot themselves. The book achieved a million copies in sixteen editions in Germany, along with editions in France and England: it reached as far as China: it was dramatised, plagiarised, parodied and imitated – a sensation.

Having achieved his million sales-figure, Goethe remarked, fairly gracelessly, that it was absurd for anyone to write for a sale of less, and, having written his novel in four weeks, he then took one week over his next work for the stage, which he then declared was the exact and ideal time it should take to write a play – his days were not yet organised to let him work on several things at one time, as they were later.

In the play, which occupied Goethe, we must assume, for rather more than the week he claimed to have spent on it, we find, in Clavigo and Carlos, the first of the double-portraits which culminate in the two souls that wrestle for dominion in the breast of Faust. The events described in the play had actually happened only a very short time before the play was written. In 1773, the story had appeared for the first time, in Beaumarchais' memoirs, written to defend the author in a lawsuit: several documents are taken up verbatim in the play's text: the characters in the play who survive the last act and even the title role, who does not, were still all very much alive and well, living in Madrid, out of the reach of libel suits. It is not hard to see what attracted Goethe to the story: the hero a writer, behaving with the carelessness of genius, prompted by a cleverer less conscientious friend, a girl abandoned not once but twice. (Incidentally, Goethe must be congratulated here, for once, on his moderation. In fact, Clavigo let Marie down no less than three times, a development which would have been dramatically implausible, to say the very least.) The ambiguity of Goethe's presentation of Clavigo is new and interesting. Is Clavigo the hero or the villain?

A figure who falls at the end of a tragedy is not necessarily the hero of it, merely the victim; in this case, the casualties both seem more passive than active. The play's ending shows no one in a winning light, a fact that makes it all the more performable today, when such ambiguities only add to a play's appeal. Compared with some justification, to Schiller's *Kabale Und Liebe*, with its cut-and-dried morality, *Clavigo* is far the more interesting, despite its rather overblown posturing of Romanticism – the theatre of the exclamation mark.

In the present translation some of this rather lurid attitudinizing, and much of the very lurid punctuation, has been revised or removed, leaving the listener to determine the stress in a script that might otherwise sound like an extract from Queen Victoria's diary. Other excisions include one or two supernumerary characters, and one, Sophie's husband, of perhaps rather more importance, but nevertheless expendable except as a purveyor of information which others can give just as well, while Sophie becomes marginally more interesting as a widow. Also a Horatio-style 'hero's friend', originally wasted prodigally on one scene, has been subsumed into the now more rewarding part of Buenco. But these are businesses of an entirely practical, theatrical kind, which one can only hope will give currency to the first performable play by a great writer – what would we think of Shakespeare if he were represented only by *The Two Gentlemen of Verona*?

RDM

Characters

CLAVIGO
Archivist Royal

CARLOS
his friend

BEAUMARCHAIS

MARIE BEAUMARCHAIS
his younger sister

SOPHIE GUILBERT
his elder sister

BUENCO

This translation was written for, and first performed by the Citizens' Company, Glasgow, on 21 October 1999, with the following cast:

CLAVIGO, Brendan Hooper

CARLOS, Derwent Watson

BUENCO, Jay Manley

BEAUMARCHAIS, Andrew Joseph

SOPHIE, Candida Benson

MARIE, Katharine Burford

Director, Robert David MacDonald

Assistant Director, Geoffrey Cauley

Designer, Philip Witcomb

ACT ONE

Scene 1

CARLOS: The magazine will have an excellent effect. The ladies will be enchanted.

CLAVIGO: Tell me, Carlos, do you not feel *The Thinker* is now one of the leading weeklies in Europe?

CARLOS: At any rate, we have no authors in Spain at the moment who combine such power of thought and imagination with such a brilliant and easy style.

CLAVIGO: Oh, please! I have had to become the creator of good taste among the people.

CARLOS: People are willing to accept every sort of impression.

CLAVIGO: I have a certain reputation, a certain credit among my fellow-citizens; and between you and me, my field widens daily; my feelings expand, and my style attains both greater truth and strength.

CARLOS: Good, Clavigo! But, don't take this amiss, I liked your writing a lot more when you were doing it at the feet of Marie, when that dear creature had some influence over you. Everything had a more, I don't know, flourishing, youthful appearance.

CLAVIGO: Those were good days, Carlos, and now they are over. She had, it is true, a considerable share in the applause the public gave me right from the very beginning. But, Carlos, in the long run, one soon gets tired of women; anyway, were not you the first to approve my decision, when I decided to leave her?

CARLOS: You would have become morose. Women are in the end monotonous. Only, it seems to me, it is now time you started looking around for some other plan – it does no good, treading water in this way.

CLAVIGO: My plan is the court, and there is no let-up from work there. For a stranger, with neither rank nor name, not to mention fortune, have I not done well enough? Among a crowd of people where it is something of an achievement to get oneself noticed at all? I feel a considerable satisfaction at the way I have cleared for myself. Favoured by the first in the kingdom, honoured for my knowledge and my talent! Archivist Royal! Carlos, that is the spur; I would be nothing, if I merely stayed what I am! Onward and upward! And that means effort and craft. One needs a whole mind. And women? You can waste a deal too much time on them.

CARLOS: It is your own silly fault. I cannot live without women, but they never get in my way. Nor do I go in for compliments, sensitivity and what not; that's why I have as little as possible to do with respectable girls. One soon runs out of conversation; one slopes around with them for a while, and no sooner do things begin to be interesting, than the devil is abroad with talk and promises of marriage, which I avoid like the plague. Penny for them?

CLAVIGO: I cannot get rid of the thought that I abandoned Marie – went behind her back, call it what you like.

CARLOS: Marvellous! As I see it, we only live once in this world, only enjoy these strengths, these views, once, and whoever does not use them to best advantage is a fool. As for marriage! Just at the moment when life gets into its swing, to settle down domestically, limit oneself when not even half one's journey is behind one, when one has not made half one's conquests! Loving Marie was natural, promising to marry her was stupid, and keeping your word would have been insane.

CLAVIGO: I really did love her, she attracted me, she held me, and when I sat at her feet, I swore to her, to myself, that things would always be like that, that I would belong to her, as soon as I had a position... And now, Carlos!

CARLOS: Time enough, when you are a made man, when you have achieved the objective you desire, for you to crown your happiness and consolidate your position, to look about to make a clever marriage and connect yourself to a respected and wealthy family.

CLAVIGO: She has vanished! Utterly vanished from my heart! Were it not for the fact that now and then her misfortune comes into my mind... How changeable we are!

CARLOS: I'd be astonished if we were anything else. Doesn't everything in the world change? Why should our passions be the only exception? Don't worry, she's not the first girl to have been jilted, and certainly not the first to console herself. If you take my advice, the young widow over by...

CLAVIGO: You know I dislike that sort of suggestion. If an episode doesn't come of its own accord, it doesn't get my attention.

CARLOS: We are of course speaking of the sensitive.

CLAVIGO: Never mind that now, and don't forget, our main business at the moment, is to make ourselves indispensable to the new minister. The fact that Whal is giving up the governorship of the Indies is an irritation for us. I'm not worried much beyond that; his influence is still there – Grimaldi and he are friends, and we can fawn and curtsey...

CARLOS: And think and do just as we please...

CLAVIGO: That is the main thing in life. I must see this taken to the printers.

CARLOS: Shall we see you this evening?

CLAVIGO: Unlikely. Ask later.

CARLOS: I would really like to enjoy myself this evening. I have to work the whole afternoon. Nothing to be done about that.

CLAVIGO: Never mind. If we didn't work for so many, we wouldn't be so much better than they are.

(*Exeunt.*)

Scene 2

BUENCO: Bad night?

SOPHIE: I told her yesterday. She was so relaxed and happy, chattering away till gone eleven, then she was overheated, couldn't sleep, so today she's all out of breath again, and been crying all morning.

MARIE: If only our brother would come. He's two days past the date.

SOPHIE: Just be patient, Pierre won't fail us.

MARIE: I long to see this brother of ours, my judge and saviour. I can hardly remember him.

SOPHIE: I can quite clearly. He was a keen, open, fine boy just in his teens when Father sent us here to Spain.

MARIE: You read the letter he wrote when he heard of my misfortune. 'If you are guilty expect no forgiveness, add to your shame the burden of a brother's contempt and a father's curse. If you are innocent...oh, then every possible burning vengeance shall fall on the betrayer's head!' – I'm trembling. Not for me, I am innocent before God – oh, my friends, you must... I don't know what I want! Oh, Clavigo!

SOPHIE: You're not listening!

MARIE: I just want quiet! No, I don't want to cry. I have no more tears. Why tears, anyway? I'm only sorry to be souring life up for you. Basically, what am I complaining about? Clavigo's love gave me great joy, perhaps more than mine gave him. And now? What does it matter? What does it matter to a girl if her heart breaks?

BUENCO: For Heaven's sake, Señorita!

MARIE: If her heart consumes itself and her wretched young life? If it's all the same to him... Oh, why aren't I even nice any more? But he should pity me! That the poor girl, he made himself so necessary to, should have to weep and wail her life away without him. – Pity! I don't want pity from him.

BUENCO: If I could just teach you to despise that man, that unworthy, hateful...

MARIE: No, he is not unworthy; and do I have to despise what I hate? – Yes, sometimes, I can hate him, sometimes, when the Spanish spirit takes over. We ran into him lately, and the sight of him brought full, warm love back to me; then we came home, and his behaviour struck me, the calm, cold glance he threw me, by the side of his splendid Doña: at that point I became a Spaniard to the core; I felt for my dagger, took down a bottle of poison and donned my disguise. You are astonished, Buenco? All in my mind, of course.

SOPHIE: Silly girl.

MARIE: The power of imagination showed me him lavishing all the friendliness, all the humility with which he had poisoned me, at the feet of his new love – I aimed at the traitor's heart! Ah, Buenco! Suddenly the nicely brought-up French girl was back again, knowing nothing of love philtres and daggers of vengeance. We are a terrible set! Comedies to keep our lovers amused, fans to punish them, and when they are faithless…? – Sister, what do you do in France, when lovers are untrue?

SOPHIE: You put a curse on them.

MARIE: And then?

SOPHIE: And then? You let them go.

MARIE: Why should I not let Clavigo go? If that is the fashion in France, why not in Spain? Why should a Frenchwoman in Spain not be a Frenchwoman? We'll let him go and find another; it seems that's how they carry on here too.

BUENCO: He broke a solemn promise, not some novelettish frivolity, or some social *attachement*. Mademoiselle, you have been insulted in your inmost being. Oh, never has my social position as a simple citizen of Madrid been so irksome as it is now, making me so weak, so incompetent to demand justice for you against that false courtier.

SOPHIE: Who is that now? Send them away, Buenco, will you?

MARIE: When he was still just Clavigo, not yet the Archivist Royal, when he was the stranger, the new arrival, just introduced into our house, how kind he was, how nice! All his ambition, all his aspirations seemed to be the product of his love! It was for me that he struggled for rank, name, property: now he has them, and I...!

BUENCO: Your brother is here.

SOPHIE: Pierre!

MARIE: Where? Where? Take me to him!

BEAUMARCHAIS: (*Entering.*) Sister! My sister!

MARIE: Is it you? God be thanked, it is!

BEAUMARCHAIS: Let me come to myself.

MARIE: Oh, my poor heart!

SOPHIE: Calm yourselves! Dear brother, I had hoped to see you more relaxed.

BEAUMARCHAIS: Relaxed! Is that what you are, relaxed? You mean I am not seeing, in the worn features of this dear child, in your pallor of concern, in the silence of your friend, that you are as wretched as I have been imagining you the whole, long way here?

SOPHIE: And Father?

BEAUMARCHAIS: He will bless you and me, if I can save you.

BUENCO: Señor, if you will permit a comparative stranger, who recognises your worth and nobility at first glance, to lay bare his feelings about this whole business! You have made this lengthy journey to save your sister, to avenge her. Be as welcome as an angel, even if you put us all to shame.

BEAUMARCHAIS: I hoped, Señor, to find hearts in Spain like your own; that is what spurred me on to take this step. Nowhere in the world is there a lack of sympathetic, applauding souls, the moment someone appears, whose circumstances give him total freedom to follow what he is determined on. Everywhere there are noble men among the great and powerful, and the ear of Majesty is seldom deaf: it is our voices that are often too weak to reach so high.

SOPHIE: Come, sister! Come! Lie down for a while. She is utterly exhausted.

MARIE: Brother!

BEAUMARCHAIS: Pray God you are innocent, and then, every vengeance on the traitor. Brother! Let me come to myself. And then! A clear, unprejudiced examination of the whole matter. It will affect my actions. The feeling of a just and good cause will reaffirm my resolve; and believe me, if we are in the right, we shall have justice.

ACT TWO

CLAVIGO: Who might the Frenchman have been who had himself announced? French! At any other time, that nation would have been welcome to me! – why not now! It is extraordinary that the superior man should be hobbled by a thread in this fashion – tcha! – was I more guilty towards Marie than myself? – is it my duty to make myself unhappy because a girl is in love with me? (*Exit.*)

BEAUMARCHAIS: (*Entering.*) I feel so easy! So well! Friend, I am here at last, I have him; he shall not escape me.

BUENCO: Stay calm; at least show him the appearance of relaxation.

BEAUMARCHAIS: My sister! My sister! Who would have believed that you could be as blameless as you were unhappy?

BUENCO: It will come to light, you will be avenged.

BEAUMARCHAIS: And merciful God, keep me in this calmness of mind in which you have set me at this moment, so I may act with moderation and negotiate as cleverly as possible.

BUENCO: This cleverness, everything you have ever shown in the way of moderation, I shall take upon myself. Though once more, I urge you to have some consideration for where you are: in a strange country, where all your protectors, all your money, is of no use in ensuring you against the machinations of unworthy enemies.

BEAUMARCHAIS: Have no fear. Play your part well, and there is no reason for him to know which of us he has to deal with. I am in a humour to cook him on a slow fire.

CLAVIGO: (*Re-enters.*) Gentlemen, it is a pleasure for me to welcome citizens of a nation I have always admired.

BUENCO: Señor, I trust and hope we shall be worthy of the honour that you are kind enough to do our compatriots. The prospect of making your acquaintance overcame the concern we felt that we might incommode you.

CLAVIGO: Those whom the first glance recommends, should not drive modesty to such lengths.

BUENCO: Clearly it can be no novelty to you to be visited by strangers, since you have made yourself as well known in other countries, for the excellence of your writings, as the offices bestowed on you by His Majesty have made you in your own.

CLAVIGO: The King has shown much honour to my unworthy services, and the public much forbearance towards the trifling productions of my pen; I could wish that I might contribute in some way towards the improvement of taste in my country, and the expansion of knowledge. For that is what binds us to other nations, makes us friends with the most distant spirits, and forges the most comforting links with those who, alas, are prevented by *raison d'état* from making other contact.

BUENCO: It is a pleasure to hear the opinions of a man who has a like influence both on the state and the sciences.

BEAUMARCHAIS: I must confess, you took the words out of my mouth, and bring me directly to the subject which brings me here. A society of eminent, scholarly men entrusted me with the mission, that wherever my travels took me, where I found opportunity, I should establish a correspondence between them and the best heads of the kingdom in question. As currently no Spaniard writes better than the author of those pages that circulate under the celebrated name of *The Thinker*, a man I have the honour of speaking to... I think I cannot render my friends a more suitable service than in bringing them together with such a man.

CLAVIGO: No suggestion in the world could be more welcome to me, gentlemen. Not that I can satisfy the wishes of your learned friends; that far my vanity does not carry me. I have till now seen myself as a purveyor, who has the slim virtue of making the discoveries of others available to the community at large. But thanks to your intervention, I am become the middleman, who has the good fortune of spreading the fame of his own country, and enriching it with treasures from abroad. So you will allow me, gentlemen, not to treat the bringer of such comforting news as a stranger. Allow me to ask him what is the request that has brought him this long distance? Not that I would permit myself such an indiscretion to satisfy a vulgar curiosity: no, rather believe that it occurs in the purest intention of employing for you every capacity, every influence I may possess: for I must inform you, you have arrived at a place where the stranger may expect to encounter innumerable vicissitudes in the successful performance of his affairs, especially at court.

BEAUMARCHAIS: I embrace such a generous offer. I have no secrets from you, Señor, and my friend here will be no way *de trop* in our discussion; he is fully acquainted with the matter on which I have to speak to you. There was a French merchant, with a large number of children and a consequently modest fortune, who had many business correspondents in Spain. One of the richer of these, passing some nine or ten years ago through Paris, made him the following proposition. 'Let me take two of your daughters to Madrid with me, and look after them. I am unmarried, of a certain age, without family. They would be the comfort of my old age, and after my death they will inherit one of the most prosperous business houses in Spain.' The eldest, already married, and one of the younger sisters were entrusted to him; the father undertook to supply the firm with all the French goods which it needed, and so everything looked rosy, until the correspondent suddenly died, having failed to settle a farthing on the two French girls, who were thus in the unfortunate position of having to run a business on their own. The elder was recently widowed, and despite lack of fortune, their exemplary behaviour and characters won them a host of friends, who vied with one another in expanding both their business and their credit. Round about this time, a young man, a native of the Canary Islands, had himself introduced to the house. Despite his lack of fortune – and position – the young women took to him. Full of the desire to make a name for himself, he hit on the idea of giving Madrid the pleasure, a new one for the nation, of a weekly periodical on the pattern of the *Spectator* in England. From his two friends he received encouragement and assistance of every kind. There could be little doubt that such an enterprise would be rewarded with every success. And so, encouraged by the prospect of soon becoming a person of some consequence, he dared openly to propose marriage to the younger of the two French girls. They gave him hope. 'Begin,' said the elder, 'by succeeding; and when some office, or favour at court, or some other means of existing honourably, presents itself, and if she should prefer you to other suitors, then I shall see no reason to withhold my permission.' The younger sister rejected several advantageous offers, her feelings of attraction for the young man helping her to bear the worries of an uncertain wait; she interested herself in his good fortune as if it had been her own and encouraged him to bring out the first issue of his periodical, under the promising title of *The Thinker*. The work achieved an astonishing success; the King himself gave the author public indications of his approval. He was promised the next worthwhile appointment that should present itself. From that moment he set all rivals for the lady at a distance, and paid her public attention. The wedding was delayed only by the waiting for the promised promotion. – Finally, after six years, the appointment appeared – and the young man disappeared. The affair had excited too much notice for anyone to observe the development with indifference. The whole town was talking of it. The young ladies turned to powerful protectors; only the unworthy creature, by now familiar with the intrigues of the court, was able to draw the teeth of all their efforts, going so far in his insolence as to dare to threaten the poor girl, and say to her friends who came to confront him, to their faces, that the Frenchwomen should be on their guard if they were thinking of proceeding against him, as it would be easy enough for him to ruin them since they were in a foreign country without help or support. At this news, the poor girl fell into convulsions; her life was feared for. In despair the elder sister wrote to France; the report moved their brother terribly, and he demanded immediate leave of absence to investigate such a confused business for himself, journeying without stopping to Spain. I come, therefore, armed with the cause of right and with the determination to unmask the betrayer, and that is – you!

CLAVIGO: Listen, Señor… I am… I have…there doubtless is some…

BEAUMARCHAIS: Do not interrupt. You have nothing to say to me, and much to hear. To begin with, have the goodness to make a declaration before this gentleman, who is here with me for that express purpose, whether my sister, by any sort of infidelity, frivolity, weakness, misbehaviour, or any other fault whatever, has deserved this public affront you have put upon her.

CLAVIGO: No, Señor. Your sister, Doña Maria, is a woman of spirit, grace and virtue.

BEAUMARCHAIS: Has she ever since your acquaintance with her, given you an opportunity to complain of or think less of her?

CLAVIGO: Never.

BUENCO: In which case, what sort of monster are you, to have the cruelty to torment the girl almost to death? Simply because she preferred your heart to ten others, all of whom exceeded you in honesty, and some in fortune.

CLAVIGO: Oh, Señor! If you only knew, how I was beset on all sides…ill-advised…how circumstances…

BEAUMARCHAIS: Enough! You have heard the justification of my sister – now go and publish it. What remains for me to say to the gentleman does not need a witness. Sit down! Sit down! Since we have come this far, I am going to make you a suggestion, with which I hope you will be in agreement. It chimes neither with your arrangements nor with my own, that you should marry my sister; nor have I come here as the brother from a comedy, to make a happy ending and a find a husband for her. You have cold-bloodedly insulted an honest girl, because you thought that, in a foreign country, she would find neither support nor revenge. That is the behaviour of a scoundrel and coward. Therefore, of your own free will, with your doors open and your staff present, who will not understand you, as we shall be speaking French, you will declare that you betrayed, deceived and outraged my sister without the slightest cause; with this declaration in my hand, I shall go to Aranjuez, where our ambassador is currently residing, I shall show it to him, I shall have it published and the day after tomorrow the court and the city will be fully acquainted with it. I have powerful friends here, I have time, and I have money, all of which I shall apply to your persecution until the anger of my sister is appeased, and she herself bids me desist.

CLAVIGO: I shall make no such declaration.

BEAUMARCHAIS: In your position I might find myself similarly disinclined. But this is the reverse of the medal; if you do not write it, I shall from this moment not leave you; I shall go wherever you go, until, wearied of such company, you attempt to rid yourself of it by force of arms. If I prove luckier than you: without seeing the ambassador, or anyone here, I shall take my dying sister and return with her to France. If Destiny is kind to you, I shall have done my duty; I have made my will already, and you will have had all the advantages over us and will be able to laugh at our expense. Now please order breakfast! I shall be in the gallery next door.
(*Exit.*)

CLAVIGO: Air! I must have air! – that surprised you then, Clavigo, being treated like a naughty boy! – how are you going to put an end to this terrible situation? Into which you have been thrown by stupidity and treachery! Ha! Short and sweet! And would there be no other way, no other means but death? Or murder? – To rob the unhappy girl of her last comfort, her only support, her brother! – and to bring on myself the double, insupportable curse of a ruined family! Oh, that was not the way things looked when the sweet creature first attracted you with such charm. And when you abandoned her, why did you not see the cruel consequences of your misdeed? – what happiness awaited you in her arms! In the friendship of such a brother! – Oh, if you could only forgive me! Marie! If I could just weep away my guilt at your feet! And why not? Señor!

BEAUMARCHAIS: (*Enters.*) What have you decided?

CLAVIGO: Monsieur de Beaumarchais, listen to me. Nothing in the world can excuse my behaviour towards your sister. Ambition undid me. I was afraid my plans for my chances of fame would have been brought to nothing. Had I had any idea that she had a brother like yourself, she would have ceased to be an unimportant foreigner in my eyes. I should have hoped for considerable advantages from such a union. In making my fault apparent in this fashion, Señor, you have awakened the desire, and given me the strength to repair any breach I may have committed. I am at your feet. Give me your sister again, Señor, and I shall think myself utterly happy to receive at your hand both a wife and a pardon for all my faults.

BEAUMARCHAIS: My sister no longer loves you, and I despise you. Just write the declaration I asked for, and leave me the concern of finding a suitable revenge.

CLAVIGO: Your stubbornness is neither just nor wise. I admit it is hardly for me to try to repair such a murky affair. That depends on the heart of your admirable sister, whether she wishes to set eyes on a wretch, who does not deserve to see the sunlight again. All your duty, monsieur, is to examine that question and afterwards go along with her decision if it does not appear to be a youthful thoughtless heated action. If Doña Maria proves merciless, then it will be time, Señor.

BEAUMARCHAIS: I must insist on the declaration.

CLAVIGO: And if I were to challenge you?

BEAUMARCHAIS: Good, Señor. Well and good.

CLAVIGO: One word more. You have right on your side. Let me provide wisdom. Have a care for what you are doing. In any case we are both lost irretrievably. If I should rob Marie of her brother I should complete her misfortunes…but the murderer of Clavigo would never regain the frontier.

BEAUMARCHAIS: The declaration, Señor, the declaration!

CLAVIGO: So be it, then. I shall write the declaration, at your dictation. Only promise me not to make use of it before I have had the chance to convince Doña Maria of my changed, penitent heart; been able to say a word to your elder sister, before she has the chance to put in a good word for me with my love. Good day, Señor.

BEAUMARCHAIS: I am going to Aranjuez.

CLAVIGO: Very well, until your return, the declaration can stay in your pocket; if I do not attain my pardon, your vengeance may have free rein. If you reject this suggestion, it will become a matter of life and death between the two of us. And the victims of such over-hastiness, whatever the outcome, will always be yourself and your unfortunate sister.

BEAUMARCHAIS: How fitting you should feel such pity for one you made so miserable.

CLAVIGO: Then you are content?

BEAUMARCHAIS: I shall give in; but I shall return from Aranjuez, make inquiry and hear the truth. Should you not have been forgiven, then straight to the printers' with the declaration!

CLAVIGO: How would you like it?

BEAUMARCHAIS: In the presence of your servants!

CLAVIGO: Why?

BEAUMARCHAIS: Just give order for them to assemble in the adjoining gallery. I do not want it said that I forced you.

CLAVIGO: How thoughtful!

BEAUMARCHAIS: I am in Spain and I am dealing with you.

CLAVIGO: So be it. Call the staff together and have them wait in the gallery. Now, shall you leave the wording to me?

BEAUMARCHAIS: I shall not. Write what I say. 'I, the undersigned Joseph Clavigo, Archivist Royal...confess that during the time that I was accepted in friendship in the house of Madame Guilbert...I betrayed Mademoiselle de Beaumarchais, her sister, with repeated offers of marriage...'

CLAVIGO: Señor...

BEAUMARCHAIS: You have another word for it?

CLAVIGO: I would think...

BEAUMARCHAIS: '...betrayed! I abandoned her, without any fault or weakness on her side being either reason or excuse for such conduct.'

CLAVIGO: Well!

BEAUMARCHAIS: 'I recognise that I have publicly insulted this virtuous young woman; and I therefore beg forgiveness from her, however unworthy I may feel myself to be of obtaining it.' Write! – 'This confession is made of my own free will, uncompelled, with the particular promise that should this not be to the satisfaction of the injured party, I promise any other form of reparation she may desire. Given under my hand at Madrid, in the presence of her brother.' And date it.

CLAVIGO: Monsieur, you will keep your word and delay your revenge. It is solely this hope has made me write this demeaning letter, which nothing would otherwise have made me do. But before I dare to present myself to Doña Maria, I have resolved to give someone the task of pleading my cause to her; and that someone is you.

BEAUMARCHAIS: Do not even imagine it.

CLAVIGO: At least inform her of the bitter, heartfelt repentance you have seen in me. That is all, really all, I beg of you, do not reject me, or I shall have to find another, less eloquent, pleader in my cause. And you owe her a recital of the true story. Tell her how you found me.

BEAUMARCHAIS: Good, that I can do, and will. So, goodbye!
(*Exit.*)

CLAVIGO: Farewell! How quickly, unexpectedly, one changes one situation for another! That declaration, I should never have given it! It came like a thunderclap. So quickly, so unexpectedly!

CARLOS: Who was your visitor? The whole house is in an uproar, what's going on?

CLAVIGO: Marie's brother.

CARLOS: I thought as much. That dog of an old servant who used to be at the sister's, was just gossiping to me, about having known since yesterday he was expected. He was here?

CLAVIGO: An estimable young man.

CARLOS: We'll soon be rid of him. I was thinking on my way over. – What happened? A challenge?

CLAVIGO: He demanded a declaration that his sister had given me no reason for changing.

CARLOS: And you gave it him?

CLAVIGO: I thought it for the best.

CARLOS: Good, good! Nothing else?

CLAVIGO: He was determined on the declaration or a duel.

CARLOS: Who would risk his life for such a romantic gesture? Did he demand the paper with violence?

CLAVIGO: He dictated it to me, and I had to call the staff into the gallery.

CARLOS: I see! Ah, now I have you, my young gentleman! That will mean his neck. If I do not have the boy under lock and key in the next two days, and booked for the next transport to the Indies, call me a bungler.

CLAVIGO: No, Carlos, things stand rather differently from what you think.

CARLOS: How?

CLAVIGO: I hope, with his help, to obtain pardon from Marie.

CARLOS: What is this childishness? Can you not see it is a cunningly put together plan to ensnare you?

CLAVIGO: No, Carlos, he does not want the marriage; they are against it, she does not want to hear from me.

CARLOS: My dear, don't take it amiss, but I've seen country cousins in plays taken for that sort of ride.

CLAVIGO: I beg you, spare me the humour till after the wedding. I am determined to marry Marie. Pride? Don't think of it! Heaven lies on the breast of this love, as it did before; whatever fame I may achieve, or aspire to, the feeling will be doubled. Goodbye now! I must go! I must at least speak to the sister.

CARLOS: Wait till after dinner.

(*CLAVIGO exits*.)

Another stupid mistake waiting to be made.

ACT THREE

MARIE: You saw him? I'm shaking in every limb. You really saw him? I nearly fainted when I heard he had come, and you saw him? No, I can, I will, no, I cannot see him again.

SOPHIE: I was beside myself when he came in; after all, I loved him too, didn't I, with the purest, most sisterly love? Didn't his absence hurt me? – and now, the returned penitent.

MARIE: Never, never again!

SOPHIE: He is still the same gentle, sensitive heart, with the same violence of passion. He spoke of you, Marie, just as he did in the old days; it was as if your good angel had brought about this interval of estrangement to interrupt the tedium of a long acquaintance and bring a new liveliness to your feelings.

MARIE: Is that what you said to him?

SOPHIE: No, sister; nor did I promise him anything. Only, my dearest, I see things as they are. You and our brother see them in all too romantic a light. You have that in common with quite a few good children, whose lovers break faith and leave them. And the fact that he is returned, wanting to repair his faults in penitence – that is a piece of good fortune another girl would not quickly reject.

MARIE: My heart will break!

SOPHIE: I believe you. The first sight of him must have its effect on you – but do not see your confusion as an effect of hate, or reluctance. Your heart speaks more in his favour than you imagine; you do not trust yourself, because you long so for his return.

MARIE: Mercy!

SOPHIE: If I felt you despised him, that he was a matter of indifference to you, I should not say another word, nor would we ever see him again. But as things are, my dearest – you will thank me for helping you overcome this fearful uncertainty; it is a sign of deeply felt love.

(*BUENCO enters.*)

Ah, come, help me give her courage, decision, now, when she needs it.

BUENCO: I wish I could say: have nothing more to do with him.

SOPHIE: Buenco!

BUENCO: My heart turns over to think he will once again possess this angel, whom he has so disgracefully insulted, brought to the edge of the grave. How does he propose to repair what he has ruined? Suddenly thinking he can come back and say, 'Now I want her.' Why does he come back now? Did he have to wait until the brave brother arrived, whose vengeance he would have to fear, in order to come creeping back for pardon like a schoolboy? Is he such a coward? No, he will not get my vote, even if Marie's heart speaks in his favour.

SOPHIE: You're talking like a Spaniard, also as if you did not understand Spaniards.

BUENCO: At the moment we are in far greater danger than any of you think. I honour your brother's enterprising spirit; and I wish everything could have a happy end: I wish Marie should be able to decide to give Clavigo her hand, since – her heart he has already.

MARIE: You are cruel.

SOPHIE: Please, listen to what he has to say.

BUENCO: Your brother has forced a declaration from him, to justify you in the eyes of the world; I fear it will ruin us.

MARIE: Oh, God!

BUENCO: Clavigo signed it in the hope of moving you. If it fails to do so, then he will have to do everything he can to destroy the paper; he can do it, and he will. Your brother wants to print and distribute it the moment he gets back from Aranjuez. I fear if you prove obstinate, your brother will, quite simply, not be coming back.

SOPHIE: My dear Buenco!

MARIE: I shall die.

BUENCO: Clavigo cannot allow the paper to appear. If you reject his offer, and he is a man of honour, he will fight with your brother, and one of them...whether your brother wins or dies, he is lost. A foreigner in Spain! Murderer of such a favoured courtier! Noble thoughts and feelings are all well and good: but, to ruin oneself and one's family...

MARIE: Sophie, help me, advise me! Buenco, this is not true, is it?

SOPHIE: He will not dare, he will fear for his life; otherwise he would not have written, would not have offered Marie his hand.

BUENCO: All the worse; then he will find a hundred to lend him a hand, a hundred who would craftily lie in wait and kill your brother in the street. Are you really so naïve? Could a courtier not find assassins enough to employ?

SOPHIE: But the King...

BUENCO: Fine! Climb all the walls that surround him, the guards, the ceremonial, and everything that the court uses to separate him from his people, break through all that and save us!

(*CLAVIGO bursts in.*)

CLAVIGO: I must! I must!

SOPHIE: Monster! What are you doing to us?

CLAVIGO: Yes it, it is she! And I am Clavigo. Listen to me, my dearest, if you do not wish to look at me. From the moment your late husband took me into his house, a young man of no importance, when I felt an unconquerable longing for you, was that my doing? Or was it not rather a secret affinity of the heart that meant you too could not remain indifferent? And now? If a friend, or a lover, after a long, dangerous and unhappy sea-voyage, in which you thought him lost, were to return unexpectedly and lay his salvaged life at your feet, would you not take him back into your heart? Are not our passions, with which we are ever in conflict, still more terrible, more untamable than those waves which divide the unhappy man far from his homeland! How can you hate me, Marie, when I have never ceased to love you? The greatest joys in the world are never wholly without stain; who are we to complain that things have gone with us as they do with everybody else? Are we to reject this opportunity to restore the past, to set an unhappy family on its feet again, to reward the heroic efforts of a noble brother, and consolidate our own happiness for ever? – My friends, of whom I have not deserved it, my friends, who must be that since they are friends of that virtue to which I have returned, unite your entreaties with my own. Marie! Don't you recognise my voice? Can you not sense the beating of my heart?

MARIE: Oh, Clavigo!

CLAVIGO: She forgives me. Oh, Marie, my heart tells me so! I would have thrown myself at your feet, dumbly to weep out my penitence; you would have understood without a word. No, our two souls still move together as they did, when no sound, no gesture was needed to convey the most intimate movement. Marie – Marie –

BEAUMARCHAIS: (*Enters.*) Ha!

CLAVIGO: Brother!

BEAUMARCHAIS: You forgive him?

MARIE: Leave me, leave me – I cannot bear this!
(*Exit.*)

BEAUMARCHAIS: Has she forgiven him?

BUENCO: It would seem so.

BEAUMARCHAIS: You do not deserve such happiness.

CLAVIGO: Believe me, I feel it.

SOPHIE: She forgives him. She said between sobs, falling on my neck, 'I forgive him! How could he know I loved him so much?'

CLAVIGO: I am the happiest man under the sun. My brother!

BEAUMARCHAIS: Then from the heart. Though I must tell you; I cannot be your friend, I cannot love you. So now you belong to us, and everything is forgotten! The declaration you gave me, here it is.

CLAVIGO: I am yours, everlastingly yours.

126

SOPHIE: I beg you, withdraw, don't let her hear you, let her come to herself.

CLAVIGO: Farewell. Farewell. And a thousand kisses to my angel.

(*Exit.*)

BEAUMARCHAIS: All may be well, though I might have wished it otherwise. Now I have to say this was just what our ambassador hoped for, that she should forgive him and that a happy marriage should provide the ending of this unedifying story.

BUENCO: He is your brother-in-law, and so adieu!

SOPHIE: Buenco!

BEAUMARCHAIS: Don't go!

BUENCO: I shall hate him until the last judgment. Just beware, what sort of person you have to deal with.

(*Exit.*)

MARIE: He is a bird of ill-omen.

SOPHIE: He will come round in time, when he sees how well everything goes.

BEAUMARCHAIS: Maybe I was too hasty in giving him back his declaration.

ACT FOUR

Scene 1

CARLOS: When a man shows his understanding has somehow taken a holiday, it is sensible to place safeguards on him for the sake of his office. If that is what authority does, which otherwise does not bother itself overmuch with us, how shall we not do it when it is a question of a friend? Clavigo! If you are only half as manageable as you used to be, then there is still time to stop you committing a folly, which, given your lively and sensitive nature, must bring misery to your life, and you to an early grave.

CLAVIGO: (*Enters.*) Good morning, Carlos.

CARLOS: A melancholy, reluctant good morning. Is that how you propose to greet your bride?

CLAVIGO: She is an angel. They are wonderful people.

CARLOS: You won't be in such a hurry, I shan't have time to get a new coat made?

CLAVIGO: Joking aside, there will be no embroidery at our wedding. Believe me.

CARLOS: I can and shall.

CLAVIGO: Our own pleasure and the harmonious atmosphere will supply all the splendour of the occasion.

CARLOS: Just a nice, quiet, little wedding is what you will have.

CLAVIGO: Like people who feel their happiness resides in themselves.

CARLOS: It seems a good idea in the circumstances.

CLAVIGO: Circumstances?

CARLOS: How matters stand at the moment.

CLAVIGO: Carlos, I cannot stand that reserved tone from friends. I know you are not for this marriage. Setting that aside, if you have something to say, then please say it. What matters? How do they stand?

CARLOS: Lots of wonderful, unexpected things happen in life. It would not be good, if everything went according to plan. One would have nothing to wonder at, nothing to quarrel about, nothing to pick to pieces in company.

CLAVIGO: It will cause a sensation.

CARLOS: Clavigo's wedding! Goes without saying! All those girls in Madrid panting for you, and then you go and play this trick on them!

CLAVIGO: That is how it is.

CARLOS: But strange. I have known few men who make such an impression on women as you. In every family dutiful daughters are making plans and projects to take possession of you. One means to use her beauty, one her money, one her position, her wit, her relatives. What compliments do I not hear about you! Really, neither my looks, nor my money, not even my well-known antipathy to women could attract such praise to me.

CLAVIGO: You're laughing at me.

CARLOS: As if I had not already held in my hands, proposals, applications, written in their own sweet paw, badly spelt as only a young girl's first love letter can be… How many ravishing duennas have passed through my hands thanks to such occasions.

CLAVIGO: And you said nothing about all this to me?

CARLOS: I did not wish to bother you with empty whimsicalities and could certainly not recommend taking any one of them seriously. Oh Clavigo, I have no friend like you; mankind is intolerable to me; even you are starting to become intolerable.

CLAVIGO: Come on, calm down now.

CARLOS: Burn down someone's house, which he has been ten years a-building and then send him a father confessor to recommend Christian patience.

CLAVIGO: Are we to have your black moods again?

CARLOS: If I relapse, who is to blame but you? I tell myself: what is even the most advantageous marriage to him who has brought himself far enough for a normal man: but with his mind, with his gifts, it is impossible –

irresponsible for him to remain what he is. As Archivist Royal he can make himself quickly master of all he learns, and in the event of a reshuffle, he will be a minister.

CLAVIGO: I have often dreamed of that.

CARLOS: Dreams! I start with the firm conviction of not ceasing to strive until I have achieved what I intended; you could have overcome all difficulties, after which I would not be uneasy about the rest. You have no private fortune, so much the better; it would make you keener on the acquisition of one, and more careful in the conservation of it. And anyone who sits in an office, without getting rich, is a ninny. Nor do I see why the country should not yield as much to the minister as to the King. One gives his name to things and the other his talent. Then I started looking out a suitable match for you. I know several great houses that would have winked at your origins, some of the richest... And now...

CLAVIGO: You are unfair. Do you imagine I cannot advance myself?

CARLOS: Dear friend, break the heart out of a plant, it may continue to grow and grow, in countless side-shoots; it may result in a sturdy bush, but the proud, majestic growth of the first shoot is gone. And don't imagine this marriage will be viewed with indifference at court. Have you forgotten who disadvised your keeping company with Marie?

CLAVIGO: It has already troubled me, how few people will approve of my taking this step.

CARLOS: None! And you expect your important friends not to be exasperated that you, without asking them, should throw yourself away like a stupid boy throws his money away in the market on worm-eaten nuts?

CLAVIGO: That is unkind, Carlos, and exaggerated.

CARLOS: Not a bit of it. If someone does something unlikely out of passion, people understand. To marry a chambermaid, because she is beautiful as an angel! Fine, the man will be blamed for it, but people still envy him.

CLAVIGO: People, always people!

CARLOS: You know perfectly well, I am not timidly seeking other people's applause, but this much remains true: he who does nothing for others, does nothing for himself; and if people neither admire nor envy you, you can't be happy.

CLAVIGO: Whoever possesses Marie's heart is to be envied.

CARLOS: As things are, so they appear. But I admit I thought it must be hidden qualities that made your happiness so enviable; since what one sees with one's own eyes...

CLAVIGO: You want to destroy me?

CARLOS: 'How did it happen?' they will ask in the city: they will ask at court, 'for God's sake, how did that happen?' The girl is poor, has no position; if Clavigo had not had an adventure with her, nobody would have had any idea she existed. She may be pleasant, courteous, intelligent! – Who is going to take a wife on those grounds? That sort of thing doesn't last beyond the first days of marriage. 'Aha!!' says someone, 'she is said to be beautiful, charming, exceptionally so' – 'Oh, well, in that case...,' says someone else.

CLAVIGO: Ah!

CARLOS: 'Beautiful? Well, I suppose,' says one. 'Haven't seen her in five years.' – 'Quite time enough for things to change,' says another. 'One must be careful, he'll be showing up with her,' says a third. Questions, glances, theories, expectations, impatience, memories of the oh! so proud Clavigo, who never allowed himself to be seen in public without some imperious, high-chinned beauty, whose proud bosom, high colour and hot, flashing eyes seemed to inquire of the world about her, 'Am I not worthy of my companion?' letting her silken train sail out in the wind as far as possible, making her appearance still more striking. – And now the gentleman appears – and the words freeze on everyone's lips – appears with a tripping, little, hollow-eyed French mademoiselle, consumptive in every pore, even if she has for the moment plastered her deathly pallor with red and white. Oh, I should be furious, I should take flight, if the people now should get hold of me, start to question, cross-examine – fail to understand...

CLAVIGO: My friend, I am in a terrible position. I was appalled when I saw Marie again. How pale, how wasted she looks. But that is my fault, my betrayal!

CARLOS: Rubbish! Imagination! She was already tubercular, when your romance was going on. I told you a thousand times, and... But you men in love are bereft of sight or smell. Clavigo, it is unthinkable! A sick wife, who would bring the disease into your family, so that all your children and grandchildren would in time be punctually extinguished like beggars' lamps! A man, who could be the founding father of a line, which perhaps in the future...it drives me mad!

CLAVIGO: Carlos, what can I say? When I saw her again; in the first moment my heart flew to her – and oh! – when it was past – pity – profound compassion filled me. But love? It was as if the cold hand of Death had touched the back of my neck. In front of those people, I tried at least to play the part of a happy man. But it was all over, everything was so stiff, so uneasy. If they had not been so excited, they must have noticed.

CARLOS: And you propose to marry her? – Farewell, brother, and let me forget everything; let me eke out my lonely life, grinding my teeth at the fate of your blindness. Making oneself contemptible in the eyes of the world, and not even satisfying at the same time a passion, a desire! Gratuitously attracting a disease, which, by its undermining of your inner strength, makes you at the same time detestable in the eyes of your fellow-creatures.

CLAVIGO: Carlos! Carlos!

CARLOS: If you had not risen, then you could not fall. How are they going to see this? 'It was the brother,' they'll say, 'he must be a fine fellow, scared the daylights out of him, Clavigo didn't trust himself to accept his challenge.' Then some fine military fellow comes in with, 'Ha! One can see at a glance he's no gentleman.' – 'Pah!' says another, pushing his hat forward. 'Should've sent that French johnnie to me,' and pats himself on the stomach, a man probably not worthy of being your batman.

CLAVIGO: Oh, dearest friend, save me! From this double perjury, this shame impossible to ignore, from myself – I cannot go on.

CARLOS: Poor man! I hoped these youthful frenzies would be things of the past, I hoped I would not see you again in that oppressive distress, which you have in the past so bewailed to me. Pull yourself together, Clavigo!

CLAVIGO: Allow me my tears!

CARLOS: Alas for you, if you have started on a path, which you will not finish! With your heart, your ideas, which would spell happiness for a quiet bourgeois, you must combine an unhappy appetite for grandeur. And what is that, Clavigo? Raising oneself in rank and respect above others? Don't you believe it! If your heart is not superior to other hearts, if you are not in a position, calmly to put yourself above situations that would terrify the average man, then, for all your sashes and stars and orders, an average man is what you are. So! Either you marry Marie and find your happiness in a quiet bourgeois existence; or else you proceed along the path of honour, towards the not all that distant aim. But you must decide! – there is nothing more pitiful in this world than an undecided man, who swings between two feelings, wishing to reconcile them, but not seeing that nothing can do that, except the unrest which gives him so much trouble. Make up your mind!

CLAVIGO: If I just had a single spark of your strength, your courage.

CARLOS: It is dormant in you, and I shall blow on it until the flames awake. Happiness and distinction await you. I do not wish to paint the outlook in deceptive poetical colours; but imagine yourself in the vigour with which you confronted your soul, in absolute clarity, before that French feather-brain turned your senses. But even there, Clavigo, you can follow your path, looking neither left nor right. May the certainty of conviction come over you, that extraordinary people are extraordinary in the fact that their duties differ from the duties of ordinary men; that those whose work it is to oversee a great entity, to govern, to preserve, need not reproach themselves for neglecting minor details, or sacrificing small details to the well-being of the whole. If that is what the Creator does in Nature, and the king in his state – why should we not do the same?

CLAVIGO: Carlos, I am finally a small man.

CARLOS: We are none of us small, if circumstances encourage us to act, only if they overwhelm us. Throw away the remains of a wretched passion, which suits you as miserably as the little grey jacket and the modest look with which you first arrived in Madrid. What that girl did for you, you long ago repaid her; and the fact that you owed your first friendly reception to her... Oh, almost any other would have done as much for the pleasure of your company, that and more, without making such pretensions about it – would it occur to you to give your schoolmaster half your fortune, for teaching you your ABC thirty years ago? Well, Clavigo?

CLAVIGO: You may be right; but how do we get ourselves out of this confusion?

CARLOS: Then you want to?

CLAVIGO: Tell me how, and I will. I have no thoughts on the matter, have them for me.

CARLOS: Very well then. First of all, you arrange to meet the brother on neutral ground, then demand, with your sword, the return of the declaration you were forced to sign.

CLAVIGO: I have it already, he tore it up and gave it to me.

CARLOS: Excellent! Excellent! That step is already taken. And you let me chatter on for so long? – well, then. You write to him, quite coolly: you don't think it a good idea to marry his sister; he will find out why, if he will come tonight, accompanied by a friend, and suitably armed, to such and such a place. Signed. Come, Clavigo, write that. I shall be your second and – Now I come to think, that is an over-simple suggestion. Who are we to challenge an experienced adventurer? Nor does the conduct of the man warrant our considering him our equal. So listen! If I have now to accuse him, criminally, of coming clandestinely to Madrid, of having himself announced to you under a false name, in the society of an accomplice, of having lulled your suspicions with friendly talk, then of having unexpectedly attacked you, forced from you the declaration, and left you in order to publish it – that will break his neck for him. He will discover what it means to try conclusions with a Spaniard in an orderly society.

CLAVIGO: You are right, I suppose.

CARLOS: However, before the trial begins, the gentleman might still play all kinds of tricks on us, before we were able to take him by the collar?

CLAVIGO: I understand, and know you're the man to deal with it.

CARLOS: After twenty-five years experience? Just leave me a free hand; you need do nothing, write nothing. The man who puts the brother inside is clearly indicating that he doesn't care for the sister.

CLAVIGO: No, Carlos, I can't go along with that. Beaumarchais is a good man; he cannot be left to languish in some squalid jail just for being in the right.

CARLOS: Childish! We're not going to eat him, he will be well looked after, and it can't last for ever. When he realises how serious things are, all that theatrical bravado will disappear, he will go back to France with his tail between his legs, and say 'Thank you!' if his sister is given an annual pension, which was probably all he was after to begin with.

CLAVIGO: So be it, then! Just don't be hard on him.

CARLOS: Have no fear. One thing more! You can never tell how things get around, but he could get wind of it, and attack you, and the whole thing would be ruined. So, leave your house, don't let even the servants know where you're going. Just pack the bare essentials. I'll send you a man, who will bring you where even the Inquisition couldn't find you. I still keep a few mouseholes open. Adieu!

CLAVIGO: Goodbye!

CARLOS: Cheer up! When this is all over, friend, we shall have cause for celebration!

Scene 2

MARIE: (*Sewing.*) Why did Buenco leave so abruptly?

SOPHIE: It was natural. He loves you; how could he bear the sight of the man whom he must doubly hate?

MARIE: He is the nicest man I have ever known. I thought I'd do it like this? Take it in here, and have the end sticking up, it will look very good.

SOPHIE: Very. And I want to put some straw ribbons on the cap! Nothing suits me better! What are you laughing at?

MARIE: Myself. Aren't women wonderful? Lift our heads up an inch and the first thing to interest us is ribbons. Oh!

SOPHIE: What is it?

MARIE: I thought someone was coming in. Oh, my poor heart! It will be the death of me. Feel how it's beating, and there's nothing to fear.

SOPHIE: Calm down now. You look so pale. Please, dearest…!

MARIE: It feels so pressed-in here. A sharp pain.

SOPHIE: You must take care of yourself.

MARIE: I am a stupid, unhappy, girl. I tell you, it is only half a joy to have him back again. I shall not feel much of the pleasure that waits for me in his arms, perhaps none at all.

SOPHIE: Sister, dear, sweet sister! Such talk will do you no good.

MARIE: Why should I deceive myself?

SOPHIE: You are young, you have everything to hope for!

MARIE: Hope! Dreams, bold and young, sway in front of me, along with the beloved figure now mine once more. Oh Sophie! Since he went away, he has – I don't know how to put it – all those great qualities, formerly hidden by his reserve, have grown. He has become a man, and now, with a self-confidence utterly devoid of pride or vanity, he must make off with all hearts – and is he to be mine? – no, sister, I would not be worthy of him… I was not then, and am less so now. Much less.

SOPHIE: Just take him and be happy! – Brother!

BEAUMARCHAIS: (*Entering.*) Where is Buenco?

SOPHIE: He went out a while ago.

MARIE: What is the matter, brother?

BEAUMARCHAIS: Nothing! Let me go, dearest Marie!

MARIE: If I am dearest Marie, then you can tell me what the matter is.

SOPHIE: Leave him alone. Men often make faces without there being anything the matter.

MARIE: No, no. I've only seen you again a short while, but I can read every open, unspoilt feeling on your face. Something is the matter. Tell me what it is.

BEAUMARCHAIS: It's nothing, my dear souls, I hope. Basically, it is nothing. Clavigo…

MARIE: What of him?

BEAUMARCHAIS: I was at his house. He was not in.

SOPHIE: And that disturbs you?

BEAUMARCHAIS: The porter there said he was travelling, he did not know where; nobody knew for how long. Has he really gone away? Or was he just not in to me? Why?

MARIE: We shall wait and see.

BEAUMARCHAIS: Your pallor, that trembling – all proves you cannot wait and see. Oh, dearest sister! On this fearfully trembling heart I take an oath – if he fails you again, if he is guilty of being doubly forsworn, of mocking our misery – No, it is, it is not possible, not possible. – You will be avenged.

SOPHIE: It is too soon, too hasty. Be mindful of her, please, brother. What is it? Do you feel faint?

MARIE: No, no. You always make such a fuss.

SOPHIE: Drink this.

MARIE: Oh, leave it, what is the point? – Oh, all right, give it to me.

BEAUMARCHAIS: Where is Buenco? Send for him, please. How do you feel, Marie?

MARIE: Well, quite well. Then do you think, brother...

BEAUMARCHAIS: What, my dearest?

MARIE: Oh!

BEAUMARCHAIS: Is it your breathing?

MARIE: It's my heart, it stops the air getting in...

BEAUMARCHAIS: Don't you have some medicine? Do you need a sedative?

MARIE: I only know one thing that would help, and I've been asking God for it for a long time.

BEAUMARCHAIS: And you shall have it, and from my hand, I hope.

MARIE: Oh, good.

SOPHIE: A courier just delivered this; he was coming from Aranjuez.

BEAUMARCHAIS: It's the ambassador's seal, and his hand-writing.

SOPHIE: I asked him to stay and take some refreshment; but he said he had other letters to deliver.

MARIE: Could you send the girl for the doctor?

SOPHIE: Do you need anything? Merciful God, what is it you need?

MARIE: You scare me so much, I hardly dare ask for a glass of water – Sophie – brother! – what is in the letter? Look how he's trembling!

SOPHIE: Brother! Pierre!

MARIE: Let me see! I must... Oh! I can feel it is the end. For pity's sake, tell me quickly! He has betrayed us!

BEAUMARCHAIS: Betrayed us! Here! Here! Everything is so hollow, so dead in my soul, as if a thunderbolt had paralysed my senses. Marie! You have been betrayed! – and I am standing here! – why? I can see nothing, no way, no salvation!

SOPHIE: Marie! The ambassador says Clavigo has officially charged our brother with having got into his house under an assumed name, of having threatened him with pistols while he was in bed, forced him to sign a disgraceful declaration, and if Pierre does not leave Spain with all possible speed, he will be taken to prison, from which it is possible not even the ambassador will be able to free him.

BEAUMARCHAIS: Let them drag me to prison! But away from the place where I spilt his blood! – Thank you, God, you send those in the midst of the most intolerable distress, a refreshment, a comfort! Oh, vengeance! Everything in me longs to take hold of him, destroy him!

SOPHIE: Brother, you frighten me.

BEAUMARCHAIS: No swords, no weapons: I want to throttle him with my bare hands, so the feeling will belong to me, alone and utterly: I shall have destroyed him.

MARIE: My heart! My heart!

BEAUMARCHAIS: I could not save you, but I can avenge you. In every nerve I feel the longing for him. – I would for ever hate anyone who put him out of my way. Oh, Buenco! Help me find him!

BUENCO: You must save yourself! Come to your senses!

MARIE: Fly, brother!

SOPHIE: Get him out of here; he will kill his sister.

BUENCO: You must get away from here. They are after you. If you do not leave the city this minute, you are lost.

BEAUMARCHAIS: Never! Where is Clavigo?

BUENCO: No idea.

BEAUMARCHAIS: You know. On my knees, I beg you, tell me.

SOPHIE: For God's sake, Buenco!

MARIE: Oh, air! Air! Clavigo!

BUENCO: She is dying!

SOPHIE: Don't leave us, dear God in Heaven! Brother, go!
At once!
(*She helps MARIE out.*)

BEAUMARCHAIS: And leave you?

SOPHIE: Then stay and ruin all of us, just as you have
murdered Marie. You are gone, sister, through the
rashness of your brother.

BEAUMARCHAIS: Have I deserved that?

SOPHIE: Give her back to me! then go off to prison, to the
martyr's scaffold, go on, spill your blood, but give her
back to me!

BEAUMARCHAIS: Sophie!

SOPHIE: Pierre – live for us! Hurry! It was her fate! And
it is over.

BUENCO: There is a God in heaven, leave vengeance to
him. I can hide you till we find a way to get you out of
the country.

MARIE: (*A shriek from offstage.*) Clavigo!!

BEAUMARCHAIS: Marie!

SOPHIE: Too late! She is gone! She is dead!

ACT FIVE

CLAVIGO: Torches? A funeral? I am trembling in every limb. Who's being buried?

MAN: Marie Beaumarchais.

CLAVIGO: Dead! Marie dead! – Oh, have mercy on me, God in Heaven, I did not kill her! – Hide yourselves, you stars, who so often watched me leaving her house with feelings of such inward happiness, wandering through this street imagining violins and song, lighting up the girl listening at the window grill with joyful expectation! – And now you fill the house with cries of woe and sorrow! – Marie! Marie! Take me with you! They are starting the procession to the grave! Stay!

BUENCO: What is that voice?

CLAVIGO: Stay!

BUENCO: Stand back and let the coffin pass.

CLAVIGO: Set it down!

BUENCO: Wretched creature! Is your victim not safe from you even in the coffin?

CLAVIGO: Let me alone! An unhappy man is a dangerous one. Let me see her!

BUENCO: Do you mean to wake her, to kill her again?

CLAVIGO: Your mockery is cheap! – Marie!

BEAUMARCHAIS: She is not dead, tell me, I have to see her.

CLAVIGO: Marie! Marie!

BEAUMARCHAIS: That is his voice. Who called Marie?

CLAVIGO: It was I. I am not afraid of you. Nor your steel. Look here, these closed eyes, these folded hands! Thank you, brother! You have married us.

BEAUMARCHAIS: Hands off that saint, you damned soul! (*He stabs CLAVIGO.*)
Blood! Look up, Marie, see your bridal crown, and then close your eyes for ever. I have consecrated your burial-place with the blood of your murderer.

SOPHIE: Brother! Oh, God, what is happening?

BEAUMARCHAIS: Come closer, dearest, and look. I hoped her bride-bed to have decked with roses – now see the roses I strew her with for her journey to Heaven.

SOPHIE: We are lost!

CLAVIGO: Save yourself, save yourself before daylight. God sent you as an avenger, now let him guide you! – Sophie – forgive me – brother – friends – forgive me.

BEAUMARCHAIS: His welling blood quenches all the burning vengeance in my heart! With his ebbing life, my anger ebbs too! Die, I forgive you.

CLAVIGO: Your hand! And yours, Sophie! Yours too!

SOPHIE: Give it him, Buenco.

CLAVIGO: Thank you. You are as you used to be. Thank you all. And if you are still to be in this town, oh, spirit of my love, look down and give your blessing and forgive me too! – I come, I come. – Save yourself, my brother! Tell me, did she forgive me? How did she die?

SOPHIE: Her last word was your unlucky name. She left without taking leave of us.

CLAVIGO: I shall overtake her on the way, and bring your farewell.

(*CARLOS runs in.*)

CARLOS: Clavigo! Murderers!

CLAVIGO: Carlos! See here the victim of your cleverness …and now, for the sake of the blood in which my life pours away, save my brother…

CARLOS: My friend! Why are you standing there? Fetch a doctor!

CLAVIGO: It is no use. Save my unhappy brother. – Give me your hand on it! They have forgiven me, and so I forgive you. See that he gets to the frontier, and – ah!

CARLOS: Clavigo! Clavigo!

CLAVIGO: Marie! Give me your hand!

SOPHIE: Get away from her, get away!

CLAVIGO: Her hand! Her cold, dead hand! You are mine …and now, from your bridegroom, a kiss…ah!

SOPHIE: He is dead. Save yourself, brother!

The End.